MILLION DOLLAR CUP OF WATER

Discovering the Wealth in Authenticity

ADAM MARK SMITH

www.MillionDollarCupOfWater.com

I have tried to recreate events, locales, and conversations from my memories of them. In order to maintain their anonymity in some instances I have changed the names of individuals and places, I may have changed some identifying characteristics and details such as physical properties, occupations, and places of residence.

Unless otherwise noted, all scripture is from the King James Version [kjv]

Editing by Cara Highsmith, Highsmith Creative Services, www.
highsmithcreative.com
Cover and Interior Design by Mitchell Shea, www.atdawndesigns.com

Printed in the United States of America

ISBN 978-0-9961332-1-0

First Edition 14 13 12 11 10 / 10 9 8 7 6 5 4 3 2 1

This book is dedicated to my wife, four sons, and life, who have all shown me in their own unique ways that wealth is measured by more than just money.

CONTENTS

Foreward VI

SECTION ONE IX

Chapter 1 - Drowning 1

Chapter 2 - Diving 13

Chapter 3 - Money on the Wall 25

Chapter 4 - Hungry for Acceptance 35

Chapter 5 - Dating a Whore and an Angel 47

Chapter 6 - Cardboard Casket 61

Chapter 7 - DLJ LA 73

Chapter 8 - Fathers Heal 87

SECTION TWO 99

Chapter 9 - Seeker of Truth 101

Chapter 10 - Million Dollar Cup of Water 115

Chapter 11 - More to Pay 135

Chapter 12 - Thanksgiving 151

Chapter 13 - The Scarlet Name 163

SECTION THREE 179

Chapter 14 - I'm A Mistake 181

Chapter 15 - Devil Preacher 189

Chapter 16 - Masks Fall 215

Chapter 17 - The Wealth in Authenticity 225

Chapter 18 - Perfectly Imperfect 233

Epilogue 237

ABOUT THE AUTHOR 240

ACKNOWLEDGEMENTS 241

Notes 244

Foreword

This book was born in August 2013 during an *Intensive Journal*® workshop I attended during the lowest moment of my thirty-seven-year life. I needed help and this workshop provided a safe space for me to reflect on the movements of that life.

Writing allowed me to recognize the past as past, to draw upon my own inner wisdom and observe myself doing so, to acknowledge the past's role and let it go. This book was written for me to read, which unexpectedly resulted in my acceptance of what happened and what was continuing to happen. Simply, it allowed me to flow with the current of life.

More pointedly, writing this book has healed me. Writing unlocked deep truths buried under the repressed fear of seeing myself as I really am—a fear, I sense, many others experience in their own lives.

The purpose of publishing this book is to share an authentic journey of self-reflection with those who might benefit from intimately observing this process. By witnessing how another handled the suffering and sweetness of what life presents to all of us, they might be ignited with the courage to observe their own journeys. We are experiencing, paradoxically, both alone and with each other, a journey toward our own authenticity.

To be candid, I prefer to keep my personal life private. However, as I told this story to the initial few, it became clear that publicly sharing the story is an act of love that began as a private gift to myself in August 2013 in a small room of people, all of us silently writing, all of us self-reflecting, all of us, together, being alone with ourselves.

Sharing this story is what love would do if it had a voice. It is a song—what love would sing to us when we needed love most. A voice we all have within us. A voice we are afraid to hear because it can sound so alien to what we are told by our minds, our televisions, our computers, our education, our economy, and even our friends.

While publicly sharing has cost my family and me our privacy, the story allows others to connect with their own, private selves, the selves we do not want anyone else to see, the selves we even hide from ourselves at a very early age, but the selves we *must* meet if we are to show up in this life authentically.

SECTION ONE

ENDURE TO GIVE

"You wanna fly, you got to give up the shit that weighs you down."

—Toni Morrison, Song of Solomon, 1977

Chapter 1
Drowning

I gulped. Water rushed into my throat. I raised my hand.

I had held my breath for as long as a six-year-old could. I watched the light shrink from the top of the water, kicking my legs in vain as I sank in the unexpected, cold, dark hole. My wet jeans and t-shirt pulled me down in the sandy, shallow wash beneath the rusted steel bridge on that hot summer day in Tucson, Arizona.

*****

This was not the first time I had breathed water. Just one year prior, I had been out fishing off the bank of a rushing river in Clifton, Arizona, with my younger siblings and my parents. I had accidentally dropped my pole in the flowing, shallow water. I was reaching for it, hoping to grab it before the reel was knocked loose from the rock where it was hung (and hoping to catch it before my dad turned around from untangling the hook from my brother Abel's shirt for the third time). The water made my hand look bigger and the fishing pole much closer than they were.

I reached in farther and farther and … splash … in I went and was quickly swept away.

Dad had somehow heard the unique-sounding splash over the slapping of water on rocks. Perhaps it was the sound he imagined a child might make if falling into the water—the sound a parent listens for when taking a fishing trip with young children. We were poor kids and wore large, adult-sized, orange life jackets from Goodwill. The life jackets were so wide on us that it made clapping our hands together or doggie paddling impossible.

Mom was tending to the youngest children in our van parked a quarter mile downstream. Pregnant, nursing Amelia, and watching Aaron and the twins while they napped, she was oblivious to the fact that her oldest child was headed right toward her. Dad yelled, "Don't move!" at my panicking, four-year-old brother standing on the riverbank, his voice so loud that even I, with my face down in the moving water, could hear him. Dad was coming for me. When the rocks weren't covered with air bubbles from the moving, muddy water, I could see their rounded edges just out of reach of my flailing hands as I floated by. I could also hear my dad yelling, "Flip over!" or maybe that was just my mind screaming this to myself. I wasn't sinking, I was moving at the exact speed of the quick current, drifting away from my crying brother. I jerked to flip but couldn't. The current was too strong and my arms were rendered useless by the over-sized life jacket.

After what seemed like an hour, Dad finally reached me and pulled me up out of the water, stronger than it was deep. Dad's arms cradled me tightly as he pulled me to the river's edge that happened to be near our van. Dad carried my limp body to the nearest dry area while screaming, "Oh God, I'll do anything!" Dad pounded my chest with his thick, heavy, weathered 53-year-old fist, "Anything! Just please don't take this boy, too!" Dad meant it when he said he would do anything.

*****

It was 1973 and my dad, Gene (known as Gene-O), and his firstborn, Mark, were inseparable. Gene-O wasn't just a father to Mark; they were best friends. Gene-O and nineteen-year-old Mark both wore long, hippie hair. Mark hated school and left before graduating, but he loved hanging with his dad at the bar his father owned on the corner of Valencia and Old Nogales Highway—a seedy side of Tucson, Arizona, at the time. They smoked and sold weed together, drank and sold booze together, laughed together, played together, and loved each other deeply. For Mark's eighteenth birthday, Gene-O handed him a teddy bear. Mark looked puzzled and disappointed until he looked inside. Gene-O had switched the cotton with a more desirable stuffing to share with his friends: Mexican cannabis. Mark felt accepted by his dad.

Gene-O didn't worry about Mark's low high school scores and early departure. Gene-O hadn't even finished junior high school himself; yet he had still managed to fight in the Korean War, marry and divorce four women, have seven biological children, adopt two stepchildren and run his own bar, all before meeting my mother.

Gene-O loved counting his money in the bar's back office as the jukebox loudly played Zeppelin's *IV* and routinely allowed Mark to serve drinks behind the bar whenever he had to go to the bathroom, count the money in the back office, or go do "bad stuff"—Gene-O's description of the shadier side of his business working for local drug traffickers. But when the legitimate side of his business took a dark turn, Gene-O was not in the bar. He was out doing bad stuff.

A drunk was yelling and complaining that Mark's black cat needed to be caged and not walking on the bar's counter getting its tail in his whiskey. The man said he was going to shoot the cat if Mark didn't get rid of it right then. Mark loved that cat and when he saw a gun in the drunk man's holster, he instinctively reached across the bar and grabbed it. The gun slipped out of Mark's hand into the air and landed on the counter with enough force to let out a pop! Blood sprayed out of Mark's temple and from the back of his head onto the dry shot glasses behind the bar.

Gene-O returned a couple hours after the coroner had removed Mark's body to find the gory traces of what happened in his absence. The police officer told Gene-O that Mark stayed alive for seventeen minutes after being shot and shared with him Mark's last, struggling word, "Father." Blaming himself for Mark's death, Gene-O mopped up his best friend's blood and permanently closed the bar despite receiving death threats from his "employer" who was not happy he was quitting the business. Shortly after, the bar burned down, but the death threats ended. Gene never deposited the insurance money, but he got a haircut and found God through a radio show that was playing recordings of a recently deceased preacher named William Marrion Branham.[1]

Three years later he proposed to a twenty-nine-year-old woman, who had recently left Catholicism to become a Branhamite, saying, "Joan, I know we have been dating for only three months and you are still a virgin, but the Lord has told me that you are going to be my wife." They married a month later and had eight children in eight years, all of their names beginning with the letter "A" drawn either from the Bible or derived from a hymn. Gene named their oldest with the intent of starting over and honoring his new, redeeming commitment to God: Adam Mark Smith.

*****

Ten years later, my dad cried out to God, "Anything! Just please don't take this boy, too! Not this one! Please, God!"

Another pound of Dad's fist followed and this time I coughed up water and gasped in the fresh air. Gene grabbed his own black hair, let out a shriek of disbelief, and ran to retrieve the other crying kid he left standing on the bank. When Abel was collected and we were all safely back in the van with my mom and the other kids, my dad realized he had lost his wallet and glasses. He then leaned over to my mom and said, "I knew we shouldn't have skipped church today!" We were delivered to the Branham church the next week and every Sunday morning, Sunday evening, and Wednesday evening that followed.

*****

Now, I found myself drowning, again, but this time my dad was not around to save me. Dad had assumed the still and very shallow waters of the wash were safe enough to allow my half-brother Sam to be in charge of the younger swimmers. He also thought it would be okay for us to go without those oversized life jackets as well. Dad was not aware of the powerful whirlpools that can form in slow-moving washes draining the previous day's monsoon.

A fake-drowning game naturally resulted when the other boys had heard of my near-death experience and noticed the reaction they were getting from my stressed face. Moments before my last step into the whirlpool, I had pleaded with my brothers to stop pretending. Even though I knew they were joking, I was still scared that one of us might legitimately drown and Sam wouldn't figure out we weren't faking until it was too late.

I was reminded of how it felt to breathe water one year ago. My thoughts pleaded, *Please, Sam, please look into the dark water and find me!* As I felt the oxygen thinning throughout my body, I looked up, seeing now just a sliver of wavy light on the top of the water. I considered screaming in the dark, cold water but knew I was too deep to be heard.

Everything became still around me. I lowered my head and then my hands, closed my eyes, and cried in the water.

I don't know who or what pulled me out of that dark hole. My little body lay on the shore as I coughed up water again.

Later that Sunday evening my mom asked me why I looked so troubled. I told her about the second near drowning and asked her a question that naturally popped up due to the topic of the Sunday School lesson of that morning and so many others.

"Momma, if I had died would I have gone to heaven?"

"Yes, honey," she confidently and quietly answered, "you are not at the age of accountability yet. If you had died, your spirit would have floated into Heaven."

"What is accountability and when does that happen?"

"The age of accountability is when you understand right from wrong. When you understand right from wrong you must make a choice: to follow Jesus Christ or to reject him. If you accept Jesus into your life, you go to heaven after you die. If you reject him and die, then you go to hell."

Hell! I had recently heard about that place of fire and gnashing teeth, where people burned alive with their skin hanging off of their faces, screaming for but being denied even a drop of water to quench their thirst, and never dying though wishing they could. It sounded like the worst place ever to be. And worst of all, it was forever, no second chances.

I was listening to every word coming out of my mother's mouth now and asked, "When does that happen? Accountability."

"Well, the Bible and Brother Branham aren't clear on this, but I would say at about seven years of age."

Immediately, my stomach churned. My seventh birthday was just two days away. For the time being I was safe, but I was getting too close to that vulnerable place. And after surviving two really close calls with my life, I was convinced by my mother's observation—"Looks like God may be trying to get your attention"—that I needed to do something soon. I wasn't willing to take any chances with forever. So, I informed my mom and dad I would be baptized the following day.

The pastor of my small church looked a little irritated to be doing a baptism on a day other than Sunday—the day most baptisms took place in front of the congregation. But with my luck I wasn't going to delay it even a week. And, given the fact that his small church followed an unpopular, little-known, deceased prophet whose recorded sermons were played during each church service, the pastor could use the extra member, even if the member was just a child.

On Monday June 4, 1984, one day before my seventh birthday, the pastor held onto me as we stood together in a small, warm pool located under the pulpit. I clasped my arms around the pastor's left arm to hold me above the water, as I was too short for my feet to reach the bottom. Hebrews 13:8, "Jesus Christ is the same yesterday, and today, and for ever." written on Branham's sermon tracts that were lying on the floor next to the pool, affirmed the eternal choice I made in fear and hope for safety. I looked up and read the large letters from Psalm 46:10 etched in the wooden beam above where the pulpit would be placed after my baptism reminding me of the stillness I had felt in the dark, cold hole in the wash just before closing my eyes, "Be still, and know that I am God." My place in Heaven was secured and witnessed by my proud father, pregnant mother, and susceptible siblings who all would choose to be baptized by their seventh birthday as well. In the only proper way to be baptized, as I was taught, I leaned back into the water and heard, “Based on the profession of your faith, I now baptize you in the name of the Lord Jesus Christ.”

I was saved—saved from chance, bad luck, bad people, Satan, and fire, forever. This time water saved me.

Chapter 2
Diving

Shortly before my baptism we had moved into a small, old, crowded house in Tucson that had three bedrooms and one bathroom. It was different from where I spent most of my youth.

Our previous home was an old double-wide trailer sitting on ten acres way outside of Tucson's city limits. There was no city sewer line, so when you flushed the toilet, you could quickly run outside, hear and, in some places, see the excrement move down the white, cracked plastic piping coming out of the trailer lying above ground, and out to the open cesspool about thirty feet away.

I liked living there because every day was an adventure. My parents did not like sending their kids to the public school system that did not teach about the one true prophet, so most of my days were spent discovering where our poop went, how to feed the goats without being rammed from behind, how to catch a chicken in an open space, and how to avoid stepping on the many rattlesnakes found in the southwest desert.

One day after watching the movie *Darby O'Gill and the Little People* (a Disney movie about mischievous leprechauns dancing on pots of gold) I saw a large, beautiful rainbow outside my bedroom window and fantasized about finding a pot of gold at its end. I saw it on TV, thought it must be true, and went for a walk in the desert. I had been walking for about thirty minutes when I noticed the rainbow seemed to be getting farther away. Imagining the leprechauns were moving the rainbow away from me, I started to run believing I could run faster than their little legs could. After an hour of running, the sun was setting and the rainbow started to fade. I was getting cold and looked behind me and realized I had no idea where I was. There were no streets, just desert as far as my eyes could see, and I realized that I was completely lost. I stayed calm, looked to the horizon opposite the rainbow, and set off running back in the direction my home should be, determining I would just have to learn how to drive the van before chasing another rainbow.

It was dark when I reached the trailer. When I went inside, my mother just looked at me and told me to wash up for dinner. She had so many other kids to deal with that she had no idea I had been chasing a rainbow in the desert for over two hours. Throughout my childhood my parents bragged about their success in rearing eight children. They would smile proudly and say, "All those kids and not one of them died—" the relative measure of success for a large family with a father who had actually buried a son.

The desert adventure ended when my dad's attempt to refinance the property to help pay for the burgeoning grocery bills revealed an unclean title on the land and we had to sell the trailer. When it came time to have it moved to the new owner, I was stunned to watch as men came to my home and chain sawed the double-wide trailer in half lengthwise so half of it could be hauled down the steep hill to the new owner. The remaining half of the trailer was boarded up with large sheets of plywood, and we lived in it while my parents looked for our new home.

When we finally settled in the new house in the city, we didn't have a cesspool that allowed me to track the path of my waste. The toilet was connected to metal pipes, not plastic, which I quickly discovered were buried far enough underground that even an ear on the dirt could not pick up the sound of the flow. My adventures shifted from dodging snakes and chasing poop to much more necessary and at times embarrassing tasks.

My dad broke his back when he was a teenager and it had plagued him ever since. Now, in his late fifties, still trying to work in the local mines, it was common to find his black powder-covered body outstretched on the couch. He suffered excruciating pain unable to move, let alone work for more than a day or two in a row. This would go on for weeks, sometimes for months. Shots of cortisone and multiple back surgeries did little to ease his pain.

When unable to work and stuck on the couch, my dad loved to play games— board games, cards, I Spy, 20 Questions, Risk, the "solving-math-problems-in-your-head" game, and countless others he made-up. His favorite game, though, was Monopoly. It was my favorite, too.

We'd play Monopoly for hours and hours. Sometimes we'd play the same game for days. I loved being the banker because there was always something to do, such as making change and calculating taxes. The banker is in the middle of everything, including giving opinions on trades. This role suited me well.

Monopoly is a 2-8-player game, so my dad came up with Mega Monopoly to accommodate larger groups, such as when the need for food and shelter attracted some of the older children from dad's previous marriages. Mega Monopoly consisted of nine Monopoly boards set on the floor in a 3x3 square. "Rules-on-the-fly Smith" was a nickname my dad earned and I later inherited. Additional rules were necessary for this uncharted way of playing. Rolling odds or evens at a fork on the board gave the player the option of turning right or left, respectively; he also allowed unlimited houses and hotels on properties and everyone started with nine times more money than the original Monopoly rules called for. That was my favorite part—having more money than what the rules allowed.

For one summer game we had attracted twelve players. It was the Tour de Monopoly: twenty-one days plus two rest days. Some ran out of money; some ran out of stamina. On the final roll of the final day, I landed on one of Dad's high-rent properties with hotels and saw a big grin appear on his wrinkly face. I was disappointed to have a second place podium finish, but felt I had survived well for being only ten.

As you can imagine, with an aged, uneducated, crippled father, a full-time stay-at-home mom, and never less than ten people to feed, house, and clothe, money was never in abundance. Sometimes we were poor and other times very poor. We regularly ate soup that really was just broth, sometimes with an added potato, celery stalk, or whatever was on sale at the grocery store at the time. Thank goodness for food banks and food stamps.

Food stamps intrigued me. Back then, the stamps looked more like colorful cashier's checks that could be pulled from their perforated end attached to a booklet and handed to the cashier in exchange for WIC-approved foods. It reminded me of Monopoly money.

I'll never forget one of the first times I saw my mother use food stamps. She was smiling while she pulled all kinds of food from the shelves, filling her cart with more nutrition than just broth. She placed the food on the cashier's counter, happily listening to the sounds of food being scanned and bagged. We were so hungry that my siblings and I were smiling too. However, our smiles faded when Mom realized the grocery total exceeded what she had in food stamps.

I watched the cashier sneer and roll his eyes at my mother and then condescendingly scold her for not tracking how much she was spending. Now she would have to choose which foods to give back to the store. The cashier was impatient and mean. He looked at me and I glared back at him like a wolf about to eat its prey after a long time without a kill. I told him with my eyes that I wasn't trash, that my mom wasn't trash, and that we weren't less than him. But, the truth was, I felt so ashamed and embarrassed. I wished I could disappear and hide from this truth. We were poor and that did make us trash to some people.

I learned that having money was important for living and gaining respect. Without it, I was less than, a beggar, dependent on someone else other than me.

I watched my mother's tears fall from her face onto the checkout counter as she determined which foods would make the cut. I still find it difficult to admit this, but I left my mother in line and ran to the car to hide from the embarrassment and to cry alone.

Not having enough money gave birth to shame and a need for control. This shame began to attach itself deep inside of me. But, I was young and did not know that shame could become rooted even deeper.

That lesson came on another day when we drove to the grocery store. Based on the stressful conversation between my parents I had overheard the night before, I was confused about why we would be going to the grocery store if we didn't have any more money or colorful food stamps.

Instead of parking in the front as we normally did, my mother drove to the back of the store. She put the fifteen-passenger van in park, turned around, and spoke directly to me as my siblings watched silently, “Adam, I need you to get out of the van.”

That’s all she said. I thought, *Is she going to leave me here so there is one less mouth to feed? Is she hoping someone will find me and take care of me?* I knew I was the oldest and ate more than the younger ones, but I couldn’t help it. I was hungrier. I didn’t think this was going to turn out well for me. I could learn to eat less, even complain less about the brothy soup. *Just don’t leave me, please!*

Crying, I begrudgingly and slowly climbed out of the van.

She told me to walk toward the huge, brown metal dumpster. Then she told me to open the dumpster’s side door. I didn’t want to do this because I could see in my mother’s eyes that she didn’t want me to do this either.

“Good, Adam. Now climb into the dumpster.”

“Why?!?” I yelled in protest as I ran back to climb in the van’s passenger seat, still not realizing what was happening. Her eyes filled with fear. She didn’t want anyone in the grocery store to hear me. In hindsight, I have realized this was a new low for my mother, and she had to take this one step at a time.

Sensing my fear of being abandoned, with her

arm around me she whispered, “Adam, honey, we need you to climb into the dumpster and see if there is any food in there.”

I was only partially relieved to hear these words. Shame and fear flooded into me. Shame for not having the means to get food like everyone else, and fear that someone I knew would see me in those dumpsters, but relief that she wasn’t leaving me.

If I were seen, kids would ridicule me. I needed to be liked and accepted at school, so this could not happen. After hesitating, I listened for the sound of garbage trucks, looked in all directions in case any of my friends were walking by, and then demanded my brothers and sisters turn their heads away. I slipped out of the van and jumped into the dumpster quickly, efficiently, stealthily. No one could see me in the enclosed dumpster—including me—as I closed the small, heavy metal door enough to conceal myself, but still allowing just a sliver of light through.

During the many times in the dumpster that followed, I learned how to efficiently swallow my vomit when the strong stench of rotting food filled my nostrils. I discovered that peeling the outside of a mildewed head of lettuce could reveal a fresh center, spoiled milk soured slower if kept at lower temperatures, and the chunks could be removed easily with a strainer on top of your cup. I found that mold on a block of cheese could be cut away, a molded loaf of bread was bound to have some slices that had yet to show spores, there is no use rummaging for a good strawberry in a mushy batch of them, and rotten potatoes made the soup taste funny, like it had dirt seasoning added to it.

I figured out how to forget what I was doing in the moment by pretending—pretending I was the only one in this special, dark, smelly metal store, shopping without food stamps or money. I learned to hide my feelings, push them down, like my vomit, when they came up. I donned my first mask in these metal walls. I learned to lie to myself to cope with reality. Hiding my shame and poverty seemed to be the best way to deal with the life in which I found myself. I learned to hide, well. At the time, I did not know any other way.

It wasn't all scraping the rot off of food and other humiliations; there were special moments. Getting tucked in to bed at night was one of them. My dad never tucked us in, just my mom, so her time and energy were divided by eight. This meant that my turn was typically eight times shorter than I would have liked.

Sometimes my mom just knew, as mothers do, that I needed some extra time with her, particularly on those days when she had watched me climb into dark, metal boxes. Sometimes she would sit on my bed and pull her fingers through my oily hair. Oh, how I loved her fingers in my hair. My heart slowed, my body fell deeper into my bed, and my smiling eyes closed. When I smile my eyes smile too, even when they are closed. How do I know this? Because my mother would tell me so as her fingers brushed my hair. I lingered on every nice word she whispered to me.

On those special nights I learned many things. I learned that I was handsome like my father, that I was so smart, always thinking, and I was athletic. I was the best example of being the oldest child. I believed my mother purely based on the credibility she gained from being the oldest of eight children too. I learned I was a natural leader. I learned what words of love can mean to a starving child, any child. I learned on those healing evenings with my mother what love feels like.

Chapter 3
Money on the Wall

Raising a family of ten on a fixed income of Social Security required sacrifices. Every Saturday morning, after the 6:00 a.m. family prayer, my parents would determine which kids would be spending their Saturday on the corner selling statues to feed the family. Oh how I wished my name was forgotten during this time. Having your name called meant there was no playing at your friend's house in sprinklers, green grass, eating popsicles in air-conditioned homes, and watching television. It meant your Saturday was spent roasting in the hot sun, probably alone, and bored out of your mind. If your name was called, your day started with unpacking hundreds of Mexican statues from the trailer on the corner, carefully packed in newspaper the previous night by our family after we got out of school each day. During the week, every evening except the Sabbath of course, we would pack those damn plaster statues. And every Saturday morning, unless you were lucky to have an early morning Little League baseball game, we would unload that trailer full of plaster statues, being oh so cautious not to tap the protruding wing of the more expensive $25 eagle statue against the door frame of the trailer door while simultaneously jumping down from the high trailer bed. There were mandatory job skills such as acrobatics, focused attention, packing breakable items next to other breakable items from the floor to the seven-foot-high ceilings, and price negotiations (child vs adult).

If the previous night's packing was hurried or inattentive resulting in a cracked or broken statue, the level of consequence was determined by the value of the broken statue.

A five dollar statue would likely get a response from Dad such as: "Well, people make mistakes," and a slightly disappointed shrug. A ten dollar statue would get a: "C'mon, kids, pay attention!" followed by a glare he gave to each of the kids who seemed to be the more distracted kind. A fifteen dollar statue would result in Dad investigating to find out which one of us made the mistake and which one needed physical reminding. It only took a few times for me to figure out the safest reply to Dad's loaded question, "Did you pack this statue last night?!?" was a firm and convincing stare right back into my dad's eyes and a heightened voice to sell the confident lie, "Dad, (perfect pause), I know I did *not* touch that statue last night. I definitely remember!" Of course, I would only contemplate whether I had actually lied with that statement *after* I had delivered such a convincing and Oscar-worthy performance.

A twenty-dollar or higher-valued statue got everyone in trouble. Dad's morning breath heaving in proximity to my face, sometimes a strong poke in the chest with his rigid index finger leading that tan, withered fist to barrel into me as hard as it did after my first drowning. That first punch to save my life. This last punch to save him money.

Occasionally, Dad would feel guilty enough after striking one of us with his finger, fist, or foot, and would ask, "Will you please forgive me?" No matter how angry you were, there was only one safe reply to his request, "Yes, sir." After one particularly painful Sunday morning, I was sitting in church listening to the dead preacher's voice, following along in the sermon tracts with my finger, and I just couldn't take getting hit anymore. Something swelled inside my chest. I felt like a wild animal, like a caged dog that had been poked too many times. Maybe it was the screaming dead preacher's voice that morning berating women who wore makeup, saying, "So when you see a woman wearing paint, you just say, 'Good morning, Miss Dog Meat.' That's exactly what it is. That's awful, isn't it? But that's what God thinks about it. She's just made of common dog meat for wild dogs." It sounded too much like how my dad had screamed at me just after he kicked me in the stomach that morning before church because I was lying down in the small living room's walkway again, as there was little seating area for ten people. Or maybe it was the heavy guilt I felt for pretending to be asleep the previous night while my dad pummeled my brother after smelling dried semen in the sheets of our shared bed until the boy admitted the devil made him play with himself, even though the evidence could have come from either one of us. Sometimes it's just easier being the one receiving the blow because hearing fists followed by muffled grunts from your little brother next to you never leaves your memory, ever. Whatever it was, I just couldn't take it anymore, so after the service I begged our pastor to protect us from my dad's physical eruptions. My dad received a verbal reprimand from our pastor and out of pure desperation to control eight children without the help of child protective services, "The Money on the Wall" was created.

It was a sinister system—a system of public rank and control. "The Money on the Wall" had to be simple enough for even the youngest, who was three-years-old, to understand, but complex enough to motivate the older kids as well. Each child's name was handwritten on the same lined paper we used at school, our educational paper—paper to teach lessons, to be tested, to be graded, to be ranked. And next to each child's name there was a dollar sign and then a number. It was a hand-written list of all of our names and our monetary values. When we disobeyed, instead of spanking us, my father would take away our money. Twenty-five cents for talking back, half a dollar for letting the front door slam behind us, seventy-five cents for leaving our shoes in the walkway, etc. But, sometimes someone would do something at a time when my father's back was hurting him or when he seemed angry about how much money all of us kids cost to feed and we could lose $100 in a moment. One hundred dollars! It took working all day at the corner to earn $5. This meant that I had worked twenty 10-hour days for nothing. And if I didn't have $100 or more next to my name, I would have a negative amount (debt). Having negative money meant that when dad needed a volunteer for the corner, I was going to sell statues. As the oldest, my dad already preferred me to work. He would choose either Abel or me and then maybe one of the six younger children.

So, getting in trouble meant I not only lost money, I lost my Saturday, sometimes even a school day. The school must have complained after so many absences because I recall hearing my mom remind my dad that I had missed too many school days to work the corner again. My dad would argue back, “Well, it’s either Adam goes to the corner or we starve. What’s it going to be?!” Even if my mom could stand up to my dad, I couldn’t see how starving was a better choice for me than missing school. I actually would argue against my mom sometimes so I could try to make money for the family and climb slowly out of my personal debt.

The “Money on the Wall” actually worked for a while. When the consequences of being “bad” could mean twenty days on the corner, one became very attuned to my father’s physical pain and a professional mask wearer. Angry? Nope, just kidding. Crying? Yes, but tears of joy, Dad. I studied people’s non-verbal communication—studied and admired the actors on TV. I thought, *I could do acting, I do it so well now.*

During one of my 20-day payback periods, I started a habit of crossing the street to buy snacks from the convenience store. Sometimes I got 2-for-$1 hot dogs, but most often I got king-size Snickers bars. They were the best price per ounce of corn syrup. I could use the money I would get from selling a statue to buy my sugar. I once ate five king-size Snickers, two hot dogs, two packs of Skittles, and two bags of sunflower seeds. Sunflower seeds were the best value overall for many reasons: They lasted the longest and kept my mouth always moving (fidgeting); the salt kept me drinking; and spitting seeds could turn into all sorts of games. I could put 100 in my mouth at one time, suck their salt, drink, suck, crack, eat, repeat. I'd challenge myself by trying to keep all the cracked shells in my mouth until I had eaten all the seeds, carefully storing the cracked/used shells in one cheek and to-be-eaten seeds in the other. Boredom would cause me to push the limits to the point of choking on a sharp shell, having to spit all 100 seeds out of my mouth, chug water, and then . . . repeat the challenge again. I thought, *There couldn't be a kid in all the world that had eaten as many seeds as me.* I still think I may have been right about this.

Another means of entertainment on the corner was a small TV we had. I honestly don't remember doing anything but eating seeds and watching TV through those countless days. Bob Barker and "The Price Is Right" were always on at 10:00 a.m.—my favorite. The soap operas that aired from 11:00 a.m. – 3:00 p.m. were not interesting because of the terrible acting and drawn out storylines. But Maury Povich and Geraldo at 3:00 p.m. and 4:00 p.m. were welcomed sights. I remember watching all of those paternity tests and thinking, *For real? They don't know who the father is?* I could spot the liars, but I could also see the ones who were genuinely in pain. Those were the ones I couldn't get out of my head at night. What was going to happen to the baby? Was someone going to love it? When the paternity test came back negative and the man smiled so smugly at the "whore," was anyone thinking, *That sucks, that baby isn't going to have a dad.* Did matching semen really matter that much? Was it the true determinant for whether a baby should have a father? I always wanted the test to come back positive, just for the sake of the baby. When it didn't, I fantasized that the accused sperm donor would step up and say, "I'm here for the baby, no matter what the test says." That rarely happened.

Then I started paying attention to Maury and wondered what he must be thinking or feeling. Every time I did this, the conclusion was *money.* People want to watch this drama and he's getting paid to orchestrate the whole thing. I could do that, but I would get bored.

The convenience store across the road stopped letting us use their private bathroom after we clogged up the toilet too many times and had no supervising parents to help plunge it. I asked my dad where we should go. He was angry at the clerk and told us to go to the back of their store if we needed to go. So, in broad daylight, we did.

Like dumpster diving, the secret to not getting caught was to go fast. Day after day, the poop would just pile up into a mound. Eventually, the store clerk noticed the mound and told us he would call the police if we did it again, so we had to get creative. Our solution: after guzzling a 44-ounce soda fountain drink, we went in the cup, put the plastic top back on and tossed it into the dumpster behind the store. We never heard another complaint, and we also stopped looking for food in those dumpsters.

Chapter 4
Hungry for Acceptance

I received my first through sixth grade education in a single large classroom shared by all students. The small school was run by the Tucson Tabernacle—the largest of three Tucson churches that believed William Branham was God's final prophet. Paddling students for misbehaving aligned with the Branham church's literal interpretation of Proverbs 13:24, "He that spareth his rod hateth his son: but he that loveth him chasteneth him betimes." Sometimes Sister Miles, the only teacher of the school, would have us hold out our hands in front of the class, palms down, and slap our knuckles until they reddened and sometimes bled. Other times, she would take us to her office, tell us to bend over, lock our knees, and grab our ankles, and then she would swing a paddle delivering an impact that could be heard through the walls by the other students. It was distracting for studying, but it sent the intended message of who was in control. I refused to give Sister Miles the satisfaction of letting her see me cry. Eventually I learned this got me more swats than I probably would have received, but I still waited until I was alone in the bathroom where I would kick the walls, pretend to tell her how much I hated her, and then clean my face.

When seventh grade came, my dad took out a home equity line of credit and paid a year's tuition in advance to Palo Verde Christian School (PVC), a fundamental Christian K-12 school. He paid in advance to get a discount on top of the family discount we were receiving already, which was free tuition for all after the first four kids. PVC didn't paddle students, so I was a big fan right from the start.

In our "Branham home" we did not celebrate Christmas due to its pagan origins and because it clearly had become a consumer-driven economic engine devised by the devil, which was not an issue at my old school. However, most of the fundamental Christian families at the new school did celebrate Christmas with gifts. I imagine we also didn't celebrate partly because Christmas makes poor people just plain feel bad about what they can't afford. Having been sold the idea that true love means buying the latest thing, idea, or image for their family and friends makes them keenly aware of how they aren't measuring up.

In order to conceal our situation and fit in, my professional lying had to be in perfect form on the first day of school following Christmas break. Coming to school on that first day of each New

Year was depressing. First, I had to pretend I was happy for every kid who seemingly got everything they wanted while pushing down my jealousy as they bragged of new video games, clothes, and toys, toys, toys. Their gains just enhanced my lack, and my shameful poorness—my filthy dumpster-diving beggar poorness—gnawed at me. Second, I had to lie and share my fantasies as fact, being careful not to make my imaginary gifts too lofty because rich kids can get jealous too. One time I bragged about getting the new Tecmo Super Bowl game for Nintendo—the most sought after video game at the time—and the other kids asked to borrow it. My only solution was to stall as long as I could and ended up coming to school a week later pretending to be bummed out about how someone accidentally stepped on the video cartridge and we had to throw it away. My friends were so disappointed. Some, I sensed, suspected my story to be fantasy, so I gauged their response and stepped up my disappointment to match or exceed theirs.

The true sadness was in my embarrassment and deep desire to receive gifts too. I just wanted to fit in. I didn't want to feel so second class, to feel so deprived, to feel what I was really feeling—something too painful for a proud, fragile, masked boy to see at that moment. But there was something I did feel in my body during these times. Sharp, excruciatingly painful back spasms attacked my body without warning. They happened in the middle of class, during football practice, while eating a meal, anywhere. Sometimes I would have these spasms three or four times in a single day and sometimes they would occur only once in a three or four month period. There was no clear warning, just me, all of a sudden, crippled on the floor, curled up in a ball, and gritting my teeth, trying not to scream. Occasionally I would notice my peers witnessing my pain, squeals, moans, and tears. Each spasm lasted anywhere from twenty or thirty seconds to several minutes while I tried to resist the pain and begged God to release me of it.

By eighth grade I realized that if I could schedule being sick for the first few days of the new year that was enough time for the other kids to have compared their pagan gifts with each other, gotten bored, and moved on to other topics. Skipping those first few days by volunteering to work on the corner seemed to lessen the intensity of my back spasms and was an offer my parents happily accepted.

As a kid, you find acceptance in only a few places: peers, parents, and oneself. The last two hadn't been successful for me so I gravitated heavily toward impressing friends. From being the class clown to serving as captain of the varsity football, baseball, and basketball teams, winning the approval of my peers came easily. The secret was being hungrier than anyone else—the hungriest to win, the hungriest to impress, the hungriest to eat. On the football field, it became a hunger to hit, to feel pain, to give pain.

I was the best on the team when it came to shelling out pain because I was mentally tougher than anyone. In a "head-to-head" drill (now barred in youth football leagues due to frequent concussions), two of us would lie down on our backs in the grass, forming one straight line, our helmets about five yards apart. At the sound of the whistle, we would jump up and sprint toward each other, one trying to tackle and the other trying to dodge. The mental trick was to pretend to enjoy the impact by grinning before the hit, and then immediately after falling to the ground, jumping right back up with the same grin and getting back into line for more. If you could pull off looking like you enjoyed hitting and being hit, that you only cared about winning regardless of the cost to you or them, you gained power. Eventually this drill became chaos as my teammates/opponents shuffled themselves specifically to avoid going against me. Everyone was afraid of me—everyone except the one guy even I didn't want to go against, the guy I believed truly enjoyed shelling out pain even more than I: my brother, Abel, born ten months after me. Brother against brother became the repeated match-up, the main event.

Looking back on this now, I'm saddened for those kids on the football team who didn't have the power I possessed in the incremental protective pads I wore—the pads of inner pain, of hiding, of not fitting into the box that society deemed acceptable. The other kids had no chance against me. I was decades of pain ahead of them and I literally made them feel it.

I loved playing football on my high school team. I started on defense as a freshman on the varsity team and then played offense, defense, punt return, and kick return every year after that, making first team all-state my senior year. Staying big enough and strong enough to contend in this game requires you eat a lot, and that's on top of the large volume teenage boys eat already. For most of our "away" games we had to travel a few hours each way and we'd always go to this particular Burger King on the way. It was our pre-game meal and I usually could not afford dollar Whoppers, so I packed peanut butter and jelly sandwiches from home, which was embarrassing enough, especially when the burgers and fries were just a dollar a piece. Just two bucks. Or three bucks to buy two whoppers and fries to really get full before a game. I would ask my mom and dad every time on the morning of game days if they had a couple of bucks I could have for the meal, and most of the time they responded with a no.

I never wanted to go first in the Burger King line on the rare occasions I had money because everyone could see what I would order, which was something from the dollar menu, not the extra special stuff. It was usually just one Whopper, maybe fries as well, but it was always a lot less than I wanted, and a lot less than everybody else was ordering. I didn't want others to see my shortfall, so I'd walk slowly to the front door of the restaurant, gradually head toward the bathroom, and then stall until I knew I would be at the end of the line. On days when I brought my lunch, I wouldn't get in line at all. I'd just sit at a table and open up my brown bag.

One time I had my brown bag, sat down at the table, and looked inside to find there was no food in there. I forgot to make my lunch that morning. We reused the paper lunch bags until they fell apart, so all it had was my lunch garbage from the previous day. I was so hungry and I did not have any money. There was no way I was going to ask for money or for food. I was far too proud. I got angry inside and was about to tear up the paper bag, but I decided it was best not to do so because if someone were watching they would have known that I didn't eat anything.

One of the coaches even asked me, "Are you eating something?"

"Oh, yeah. Peanut butter and jelly sandwich."

He seemed to notice that something was off, so I took the brown paper bag the way those people who drink the 40-ounce beers hide what they are doing, and I hid my lack of food. I ate my "sandwich" all covered up in my brown paper bag, except there was no sandwich. I just faked it. I faked eating my sandwich and kept my mouth closed so they couldn't see there was no food in it . . . brown bag to mouth, pretend bites, chewing on air.

My stomach rumbled and it was so painful that I turned around and pretended to look out the window behind me because I could barely hold back the tears while taking each bite. I did not feel like I could ask for help. I'm sure people would've helped. I was just so proud and I was tired of asking for help. Tired of being helped. Tired of rummaging through garbage. Tired of being poor. So I decided to fake eat to hide the reality of my situation.

I did not play well in that football game. I ran out of energy having only water in my stomach. I played terribly. And, most of all, I felt terrible that I had to fake it . . . no, I chose to fake it. I chose to hide. I didn't want to embarrass my parents. It was my fault. I forgot to make my sandwich. That's all I could tell myself. It was my fault. It was my fault. I deserved it.

*****

Eventually it became more profitable for me to work at the local grocery store with a special work permit that allowed underage, underprivileged kids to work while still in school. My younger siblings took over the statue business on the corner.

My first paycheck and subsequent paychecks went to my parents to pay for the large negative dollar amount written next to my name on the "Money on the Wall". When my ten-year-old sister slammed the door, fifty cents was the payment deducted from her name. But, at age fourteen, I should have known better, so the same infraction drew a heftier penalty. Fifty cents for her. Five dollars for me. I saw the difference even when

Abel slammed the front door. Only one dollar! My consequence was larger given my earning potential; my dad was applying a graduated tax system based on income. There wasn't much I could or even wanted to do. Quitting the grocery store may have put me in a lower tax bracket, but would also put me back on the statue corner with no air conditioning or bathroom. Plus, I saw the financial benefit to my family, and believed my earnings would theoretically trickle down to my benefit in some indirect ways.

As my contribution became a greater share of the household income, my power increased as well. For example, the supply and cleaning of my work clothes got priority, and Mom made sure I had some food on workdays. But, the dependency on me also had its drawbacks. Even when I was sick with a cold or flu and stayed home from school, I was still strongly encouraged to put in the five or six hours at the grocery store in the afternoon. So, loaded with medicine, I bagged groceries and fetched metal carts in the hot Arizona sun.

I would get to bed around 11 p.m. and be so drained from the energy exertion—energy better used to fight the infection—that I would miss another day or two of school; but I still had to make the grocery shift. On longer shifts, where a swig of medicine taken before my shift would wear off in the middle of the day, my mom made certain to send me medicine capsules to take on a break. Worked every time.

I became an investment. My value was tied to the amount of money I could make.

Chapter 5
Dating a Whore and an Angel

Being the oldest meant I was always first to try new things, including dating, which came into full swing during my sophomore year in high school. Given the lessons I learned from those Sunday and Wednesday Branham tapes of how women who cut their hair, wore pants, or put on make-up were "not to call themselves Christians, were immoral sexual machines, and were to blame for adultery, divorce and death" and "the Catholic church was a w-h-o-r-e...a harlot...the same thing as a whore: an immoral woman," I knew my dating a nice young lady in the junior class, named Amy, who did all three things that whores did, would be a tough sell. My dad was deeply disappointed in me that I had not chosen one of the "believer" girls at the Branham church who always wore long skirts, had not cut their hair since birth, and who believed in the only true path to God. It really didn't help Amy's case that her parents were divorced or that her mother had committed adultery and then remarried, which was an additional form of adulterous sin. With my dad's first four marriages ending due to the women committing adultery, he was determined that I wouldn't experience the same kind of betrayal.

"Like mother, like daughter," he would say as I waited for Amy to pick me up at my house. She had to honk the horn from the street to let me know to come outside because she wore make-up and pants. It was a house rule that any female wanting even to step on the property (my dad included the sidewalk as part of his property) must be make-up free and in a very modest dress reaching to her knees at minimum.

After Amy and I had been dating for six months, my dad grew worried that I was becoming too attached to her. And he was right. I never talked to anyone about my home life before I met Amy. But we would talk for hours, and I was able to remove some of my masks with her. With that came a freedom for which I had longed.

After returning from our six-month anniversary dinner, I found my dad in the living room looking powerful and determined to control. He talked slowly for thirty minutes about how much Amy dressed like a cunt, that she was a prostitute and I was probably committing all kinds of sin with her. Knowing what it was like to be a teenage boy, he pushed, "Let me smell your fingers, Adam. Let me smell them right now."

Fearing that a girl could get pregnant if the

boy's juice got on the girl's stomach or anywhere near her vagina, and to remain "pure," intercourse was taboo and avoided: but there were ways around it, and Amy and I had celebrated our special anniversary like many Christian teenagers who lacked proper sexual education.

Little did my dad know that I had had a relationship before I met Amy with whom I took the pregnancy risk and had intercourse one time. The guilt fostered by my dad was so heavy that it made my one experience nearly impossible.

When my dad smelled Amy on my fingers, he went ballistic. He screamed and spit through his gritting teeth, "I told you that you had a whore on your hands. Fuckin' whore. She's just a fuckin' whore! If you see that dirty bitch ever again, if you so much as look at her like you want to fuck her like I know you do, I will have a nigger go to that whore's house, climb into her bedroom window and rape that bitch while he chokes her out! You hear me, boy! It will be your fault she gets raped. Your fault!"

My fault. My fault.

My back started to spasm and then I snapped.

This was the first moment I forgot how scared I was of my father. Something burst in my chest and in my back, like a spasm but a spasm whose energy I harnessed to stand up to him. I pointed my rigid, index finger across the room, and yelled, “Don’t you touch her. And don’t you ever call her that again. Don’t you ever, ever touch her!” And I meant it with every fiber in my body. Every one of my muscles stiffened and contracted.

My father screamed, “You are the oldest, Adam, and your siblings look up to you. If you follow God’s prophet, they will follow God’s prophet. If you reject him, they will reject him. I’m not raising a son like you. I’m not having my children be damned to hell. You’ll poison the younger kids. You have served your purpose. I’m gonna go get my gun now.” Fear coursed throughout my body. He went into the closet where he kept his shotgun. I ran out of the house, down the street, and turned at the nearest corner.

Child Protective Services had been to our home many times, but up to now had only provided counseling that typically took place in a Burger King. One way to gain the trust of a surviving kid is to feed him. My counselor knew this, and when he asked how the last week had been for me, I told him about running out of the house while my father was in the closet. I described how I ran so fast on my bare feet, grateful for the darkness to shade me from my father’s aim. When the counselor stopped chewing his fries I realized I might have said too much so I concluded with,

"He didn't fire a shot." I thought this detail would make a difference to him.

The next day I was in the school office with my parents, my best friend's parents, and my school's pastor. The pastor handed us a single sheet of paper that looked like a contract. It was. My dad was being asked to sign papers that would release his parental rights of me and transfer them to my best friend's parents. I silently begged for my father to refuse to sign. I fantasized that he would break the pen over his knee, throw his arms around me, and promise to get help. I held back my tears because if he was going to take that stand, I wanted him to do so without my asking. I wanted to be loved but without having to beg for it publicly.

My father paused with the pen in his hand and then looked at me. His eyes were hollow and drained. His mouth grimaced. I stared at him like I had stared at the cashier taking my mother's food stamps. I silently told myself, "I am not trash. I am not trash," but I didn't believe it.

One vividly remembers when their father signs his name to remove you from your four brothers, three sisters, two dogs, and only mother. I was so worthless that my own father, the man I spent more time with than any other man, the man who I allowed to know me deeper than any other man, would reject me, would discard me like the trash I knew so well.

I rode home with my new family, silent, in shock, and fighting back tears. When we arrived at my new home, I went to the bathroom, locked the door behind me, undressed, lay down in the tub alone, and sobbed while the shower cried on me. We cried until the hot water turned cold and then cried some more.

A few months later I was starting to get used to waking up in a new bed, in the home of my best friend's family—a home with twice as many rooms and bathrooms for half as many people. I hadn't felt this lonely since dumpster diving. It felt surreal. I found myself wondering when I was going to wake up from this lonely dream. This fake life I was in, had to be coming to an end soon, or else I would have to contemplate that it was, indeed, real. This new bed, with this new family, from four brothers to two new ones, and three sisters to none was now my life.

I had a lot more quiet time than I was used to and spent many evenings outside under the stars talking to God . . . well, mostly sniveling to Him, wishing for my old life back but without my dad's temper. I was even willing to go through garbage cans just to live in a space filled with the noise from my brothers and sisters. Feeling poor is one thing, but feeling poor and alone is excruciating. My tears to God were real and often. My Sunday school studies taught me that I might have done something wrong to deserve this punishment. It was the only explanation that I heard, so I believed it to be true. I did this. I earned it. I asked God to reveal to me the sins that caused me this misery. I thought it must have been the time I cheated on my spelling test, the time I bullied the new kid, or maybe it was dry humping Amy. There were so many sins I had committed, so I just kept going through as many as I could recall and repeatedly asked for forgiveness.

*****

Summer with my foster family was the catalyst for my college aspirations. Summer was the time for my new brothers and me to work in the family construction business, a time when white boys shoveled next to the Mexican men. As the newest addition, I worked as a laborer making block walls in 110 degree heat.

It was a grueling hot summer indeed. At times, with hopes of escaping the heat, I questioned whether I should have taken my dad's threats seriously. Maybe, as my older half-siblings occasionally reminded me, I should have been grateful that he was relatively gentler to his last eight children than he was to his first eight. Maybe he was just angry and didn't really mean the things he said, maybe he had changed, and maybe he regretted signing those papers to release himself of me. Any thought seemed rational with a shovel in your hand under a baking sun.

Sometimes I questioned why anyone would work like this all year round. I contemplated this question over many shovelfuls and while carting fresh cement or "mud" to the bricklayers, who made $15 per hour, $5 more than the laborers, and $10 per hour more than I. Why wouldn't they want to make more money and work in a building with air conditioning and a toilet? Why would they steal a tool or a few bricks when my foster dad wasn't looking?

Two weeks before my senior year in high school, I experienced the answer in my body. I had just pushed the shovel down into the ground when my back began to spasm, throwing me into the ditch, twisting and turning me in contorted shapes. The answer was because they had no other choice. For a multitude of reasons, they were trapped with few options. I knew how that felt.

This baking summer of hard labor set me on a path of higher education. When college recruiters came to our high school, I took every brochure, pamphlet, business card, and shook every last hand. College was my ticket to a new life, a greener life that I needed to be so different from my old life.

*****

Time continued its forward movement into my senior year of high school. My dad was beginning to lose it even more. The death of his firstborn son, Mark, was heartbreaking, but to lose another son, Adam Mark, who was supposed to be his path to personal redemption, this cracked him. My dad's anger fueled more physical altercations and threats leading to more of his children finding shelter in other homes. One of my siblings went to the Myers family. The twins went to the Waters family and then the Bergmans. Six months later, a fifth child joined a different Myers family, each taken in by parents of their childhood friends.

The truth is that there are many angels in this world, angels in the form of parents whose children make friends with the Smith family and spread their wings at the moment when a child is in need, wings that catch them when they are falling into dark, muddy holes wondering if anyone is watching, wondering if anyone cares. I believe angels are real. They look like you, me, your neighbor, your co-worker. Angels are everywhere.

By this time, my rescued siblings and I had met many angels, and the day I received a phone call from the local radio station in December 1994, I realized I was actually dating an angel. The local Top-40 radio station, KRQQ, ran a heartwarming campaign called "Christmas Wish" where every weekday in December the DJs would call someone live and read a "Christmas Wish" letter sent in by listeners detailing someone's struggle and need.

I had never heard of this program, as I wasn't allowed to listen to any music containing a beat while living with my parents. A common view shared by Branhamites was that music with a beat would cause people to dance then lust and thus sin, and rock music was created subversively by the devil so he could have more followers join him in hell. My father was so against any beat that even during TV commercials, we would have to mute any commercial that had music with a beat in the background.

With over half the kids now living outside my parents' home, this would be the first year we had a chance to celebrate a real Christmas, not the kind I made up for my classmates. I might even listen to some non-gospel music with some of my siblings, as I was gradually allowing myself to listen to music other than hymns. The potential for a great memory was available. The only thing missing was money for presents and our first tree. But I was dating an angel named Amy, and anything is possible when you are so close to an angel.

I was at my $5 an hour auto mechanic job after school when the owner and his wife came out to the garage and handed me the phone. I never received calls at work. They told me to take the call in the lobby and close the door. I assumed someone, probably one of my siblings still at home, had been seriously hurt.

The person on the line asked me, "Is this Adam Smith?" I said, "Yes," and waited for the blow.

The first DJ said they had received a letter and would like to read it to me over the air, "This family has never had much of anything. Even when they were living together they barely had enough money to put food on the table. And due to their parents' beliefs, they were never allowed to celebrate Christmas. This year, I would love for them to enjoy the true blessing of a first Christmas and for one day forget about the distance between them. Thank you and Merry Christmas, Amy."

The second DJ began to describe to me what my first Christmas would include, "Hey Adam, we are going to grant your wish and we want you to have a great Christmas. We've got movie passes, so you can take all your family members out, and we would also like to buy dinner for that wonderful family of yours. We would also like to give you $100 for yourself, so that you and your girlfriend can go out and have good time. Merry, Merry Christmas and we pray that one day your family will be together again soon."

Through the tears of gratitude and the sudden realization that everyone listening to the most popular radio station in town now knew what was going on in my life, all I could muster was, "Thank you, thank you, thank you." This one phone call shifted something within me at such a deep level, a level of feeling I had learned to cover up and pretend was not there. It stirred a level of need for compassion and a desire to give back to those in need if I were ever able to do so. This shift would come full circle thirteen years later on the same radio station. But first, I had some striving to do and money to make.

*****

There's one award at my Christian school that was even grander than valedictorian. It was the overall "MVP." The award for the Most Outstanding

Christian Student/Athlete of the Year, an award that acknowledged I was worthy of others' praise, recognition, and respect—something, as I said, I seemed to need deeper than most. My teachers and principal presented this coveted award to me in front of my peers at the final banquet of the school year. The only people missing from the crowd were my seven younger brothers and sisters and my parents from whom I so desperately wanted to hear the words, "We made a mistake; we shouldn't have signed those release papers, at least not in front of you. We are sorry. We love you."

It was an empty celebration for me, about me, within me. All I really wanted was love, to be loved even if I made a mistake, even if I were a mistake, even if I didn't love myself.

As I looked up to the stars that celebratory evening, after everyone had gone to sleep in my foster home, I held the large trophy in my arms wishing there was someone to hold me. I learned that winning in life, without love, feels empty.

Chapter 6
Cardboard Casket

Unfortunately, college comes with a giant price tag. It took a lot of money to go to any of the colleges that presented at my school. Mostly private, Christian colleges. I was told I could take out loans, but I just didn't believe anyone would lend a kid without parents $120,000 for four years. "We have scholarships," they said, "As long as you have SAT scores of 1200 or higher." I had no money and no one told me those SAT tests I took actually meant something! I didn't eat the night before taking them. I stayed up until 2am playing video games, ate toast at 6:30 a.m., and never fully understood why I was taking these tests in the first place. I was just happy that taking them meant getting out of work that Saturday. No money and certified dumb, my only option was community college. Community college is where poor dogs like me went to get educated, separate from the people with money and high SAT scores, and money. I was becoming bitter.

I remember my first day of community college. I was in the bookstore and I ran into a lineman from my former high school football team. He was selling his books, not buying them. I asked him what he was doing. He kept wiping his eyes and said, "I can't do this, Smitty. My first two classes sounded so hard. I'm just going to go work at my friend's mechanic shop. I know cars." I never saw the 250-pound lineman cry during any football practice or game, even after we'd go head-to-head with each other. We both knew what choice he was making. He was giving up. His tears fueled me to never give up even when my mind was telling me I should.

Halfway through my first semester I realized I had no idea what my endgame was. Ultimately, I knew why I was attending but not how I was going to achieve what I was after. When asked by the guidance counselor what I wanted to do when I graduated, I answered honestly and quickly, "Make money. Why else would I be here? Why else would anyone be here?" She thought I needed to do more research in the career services department. And, so I did. I sat at a computer that ran a program with a database listing hundreds of careers with fields for the name of the career, a brief description of the career, how much education on average someone in the field had, and (most important) the average income of that career. I searched by field and searched by income, greatest to least:

Surgeon - $175,000 – doctorate

Commercial Pilot - $150,000 – masters and flight school

Investment Banker - $150,000 – bachelors or masters

Based simply on average income, my doubt in my ability to complete a LC Masters degree, and my previous experience as a banker playing Mega Monopoly, I set my sights on becoming an investment banker, a master of the universe, a wolf on Wall Street. Those were the animals I wanted to run with, not the poor dogs with whom I grew up. I didn't know how powerful it could be to set one's mind on an outcome, especially on one that had virtually no chance of happening.

I struggled in college and learned new things that I had never heard in my twelve years of religious-based education. At the time, I was struggling with undiagnosed and untreated ADHD and dyslexia. I studied longer and harder than most to get an "A" in my classes, believing I was just dumber than the average student.

During my first semester in community college, I realized I had to get out of there if I wanted to become an investment banker. The classes were so relatively low in energy, passion, and motivation. No one else seemed to care as much as I did about "making it." I assumed the University of Arizona campus down the road would be a better fit for my drive. With the help of federal Pell grants and student loans, I made the investment.

On my first day at the University of Arizona, my inherited religious beliefs prompted me to stomp out in the middle of my first lecture of World Religions 101, when the professor said the Bible was just like any other religious book. My first science course took me by surprise when Creationism was not taught as the origin of life. I was stunned to be taught that the Earth was not less than 10,000 years old, but instead around 4.5 billion, that humans did not come from Adam and Eve, but evolved from primates, and that other cultures had similar "Great Flood" stories that pre-dated the Bible but made no mention of a Noah, an ark, and two of every kind of animal being led into it. I would have dropped this course too, but it was a pre-requisite to getting into the business school program. So, I just answered the test questions the way the professor would mark them correct and then add the "true" answer in the margin.

My Introduction to Sociology professor found my rigid, uplifted arm irritating after he stated that intragenerational social mobility, meaning "rags to riches" within the same generation, was virtually impossible in our society. I left my arm in the air until he called on me to hear me ask, "By virtually impossible, you do mean that it is still possible, correct?" I wasn't trying to be annoying. I honestly needed him to clarify for me that the potential was there, no matter how miniscule. He eventually relented and I lowered my hand, received an "A" in the course, and kept my American Dream alive.

The only time I received a "C" in a course was in American Authors. The course was so reading- and writing-intensive that, while I learned more in that class than any other, I still only pulled a "C." I still get chills when I walk by a copy of Toni Morrison's *Beloved* or Nathaniel Hawthorne's *The Scarlet Letter.* I remember the sacrifice made by Morrison's escaped slave, Sethe, who rationalized and then chose to kill her daughter just before the posse would come and take them back to the plantation, and how Hawthorne's Hester Prynne was forced to wear a scarlet "A" for her sin, endure public shame, and then experience eventual transcendence beyond the Puritan legalism. These books came so alive for me during the course and many years after. I smile for the struggle of that course and how much I learned to appreciate details, themes, and the transformative power of storytelling. One just has to be open to seeing and receiving the embedded messages hidden everywhere.

Amy and I continued to date after high school, and, as is common for many young, conservative Christians, in order to reconcile religious beliefs and natural sexual desires, we married during my sophomore year in 1997 over the spring break. We didn't want to deal with my Tucson family drama, so we opted to fly to Walt Disney World and were married in a white gazebo in front of Amy's family. My angel was twenty and I was nineteen, and we had absolutely no clue what we were doing. But, we did know that we loved each other as much as people could at that age. The deeper reason we married is because we connected with each other's pain. Both of us came from broken homes and wanted to have a different experience. God was the center of our relationship, which gave us the firm common ground rules by which to live, a firm foundation that would end up being shaken when one of us would leave God entirely.

*****

My research for becoming an investment banker was never ending. Because I was not the only one who desired power and money, the standards were very high for even being considered for an investment banking interview: near perfect GPA, prestigious summer internships, glowing recommendations from professors, an Ivy League education, and, of course, money. Sometimes I would get discouraged that I didn't have the pedigree held by the other investment bankers I wanted to run with. But because I didn't want to live if it meant being poor, I pushed through the self-doubt and kept achieving in college.

My biggest break was landing a summer internship at Intel in 1997 in Chandler, Arizona. One of my finance professors, Dr. Moses, loved that I excelled at his tough corporate finance course. He did not allow financial calculators in his class to calculate the yield-to-maturity of a semi-annual bond and I did well in spite of that. Dr. Moses sent the Intel hiring manager, a former student of his, a sole recommendation, and I was able to put the name of the most loved public company of Wall Street at the time on my resume.

Another finance professor, Dr. Schnitzlein, thought it was hilarious that I would finish his sentences during his lectures, so he started inviting me to visit during his office hours and then eventually anytime I wanted. We talked about my investment banking aspirations. He was aware of my fundamental religious beliefs, clearly saw my drive and my hidden demons when he asked, "If Phillip Morris (a company I was completely opposed to) offered you a job that paid twice as much as Intel, which company would you choose?" I answered, "Phillip Morris, of course, just until I had enough money to feel comfortable to leave." He just looked at me and smiled without judgment. He knew he had asked a question that allowed me to see me, that allowed me to think about the choices we make when we work for companies that do not align with our deepest values.

During the Intel summer internship I received an urgent phone call to drive two hours back home to Tucson. My father's fourth heart attack was appearing to be his last. I contemplated not going, as I had only seen him once in the last four years since he signed those release papers—at my high school graduation, but we did not embrace. I felt powerful and vengeful when I walked the other way as he came toward me at the commencement ceremony. I wanted to shame him in front of the many who watched over their shoulders to see what would happen between Adam and his dad. I wanted to win and, technically, I guess I did, but the taste of that victory was not sweet. I wished the simpler days of Mega Monopoly could have been safer and more stable. I wished the beatings would have stopped at the end of the many memorable games we had played.

As I drove down to Tucson I turned off the freeway several times to turn around, wishing I had more time to figure out the mixture of emotions, including the irrational but understandable fear of physical retribution and the deep longing for a different reality—that my father and I were ending in such a separated, unreconciled place. But I was a man now and felt I could defend myself, if necessary, against a 68-year-old man on life support. My mother asked me for advice as to whether she should give her consent for the doctor to pull the proverbial plug. I tried to take myself out of the decision but realized my mother, as with the many times she stood silent as my father raged on my siblings and me, was incapable of acting on her own. I told her that Dad was a proud man and would never want to be taken care of as the vegetable the doctors said he would be if he were to live. I told her that he would rather die than appear weak. This was also my truth for myself, so the words had the power to move my mother to a decision.

With most of his fifteen children surrounding his bed at the University Medical Center, the room became still, the white sheet over Gene Gray Smith's chest raised high and his last exhale was deep. The solid line on the cardiograph gave me the assurance that he would not hurt me again, but it also held the truth that he also wouldn't play with me again—a bittersweet moment.

My dad had purchased a burial plot many years ago. The mortuary needed someone to identify the body before it was cremated. My mother said she didn't want to see her husband in that kind of state and that she knew he was in heaven because he was "a believer." She asked me to do it. I was so emotionally disconnected that I agreed to add this task to the other funerary and financial arrangements on my plate. I drove to the mortuary alone and entered a large, musty, dark room with many empty chairs. His casket was at the front of the room. People who die without money are buried in caskets made of cardboard. His casket was at the front of the room, the sides of which were partially caving in on him and covering his heavy, sunken face. I moved the caving cardboard to see his face one last time. Throughout my childhood, people constantly commented on how much I, more than any other sibling (half or full), looked so much like my dad. I stared at myself.

For an hour, I stared at myself, by myself, lying in an open cardboard box, remembering how he had saved me from drowning, cradled me, played with me, beat me, worked me, drove me, cheered me on during sports games, took just me to Disneyland, cuddled me during movies, kicked me, threatened me, smiled at me, yelled at me, told me I was his favorite and the apple of his eye, punched me, hugged me, revered me, despised me, feared me, slapped me, signed me away, asked for forgiveness, and then hugged me. Essentially, all of this was the way he knew how to love me. I swallowed, leaned in toward my dad's sunken face and whispered goodbye, turned, and left torn, confused, and conflicted throughout my being.

Chapter 7
DLJ LA

I sat in a large auditorium at the University of Arizona. I had recently won their Fall 1999 Most Outstanding Finance Senior award with a GPA of 3.9 and the support of the now familiar finance faculty that I called friends. And now I was about to be recognized as the "MVP of the MVPs," an honor awarded to only one business school senior, the business school's 1999 Most Outstanding Senior Award. I sat among my fellow graduates as we were told how we would lead the next generation of businesses. When the dean asked us to think about what was most important to us, I knew my answer. The guy next to me said it aloud. He quickly and in a low, drawn out whisper muttered, "Money." It reminds me of how Gollum would have said it, "My precious, my mm-oo-nn-ee-yy." At that moment I knew that I wasn't the only person who saw money this way. The only difference was that I was able to contain myself whilst thinking, "Get in line. No one is going to beat me." No one could survive like I could, like I had.

As I gave my acceptance speech with thousands of people staring at me, I felt their external approval, which kept me from questioning whether the source of my energy to achieve was sustainable, or was even worth the price I was paying. Money meant everything to me. It meant freedom from my past.

Even with the awards, getting a position as an investment banker was a full-time job. I wrote letters, called every human resource department at every bulge bracket investment bank, and read every book that was published about the mysterious, clubby environment. But, no one would give an interview to a nobody in Tucson, Arizona, especially someone who did not have the proper pedigree of parents, school, and network. I started to get desperate and decided that the only way I was going to get there was to fly myself to New York and bang on their doors until they gave me an interview. And that's what I did, literally. During the 1997 Christmas break, I convinced Amy to spend what little we had left from student loans on a suit and flew to Los Angeles and then New York.

I knew no one, but I knew that this was what I was going to do. I knew I was going to make more money than any other undergraduate coming out of college because I had to. I did not see any other way to transcend my past or have a future worth living for. I knew this was my destiny.

When I arrived at the major banks' front desks and asked to speak to their human resources department, they told me that I needed an appointment. I told them that I had flown out because no one was responding to my voicemails. I told them that I wasn't leaving their office until I sat down with human resources for fifteen minutes.

They must have figured that it was easier for them to give me fifteen minutes than to cause a commotion with security. Nearly every bank ended up seeing me and after feeling the energy of certainty and hunger that I emulated, I received many offers. I chose the bank that, according to Wet Feet Press and Vault Reports, paid their analysts more money than any other bank in the world, and consequently worked their analysts longer than any other bank in the world—the most money and the ability to work longer and harder than anyone else. This bank sounded like the perfect fit for me. The day after I accepted their offer, FedEx delivered me a $5,000 check and a bottle of Dom Pérignon. The bank was Donaldson, Lufkin, and Jenrette in Los Angeles, California, known by every banker simply as DLJ LA.

DLJ LA was infamous in the banking industry and full of interesting characters. When my analyst cohort began, our names and business cards were placed on a banking trophy called a Lucite, a transparent acrylic block used to commemorate a closed transaction, given to each analyst to revel in and worship ourselves. This is a very expensive way to celebrate, but I would soon learn that DLJ investment bankers knew how to make and spend money like rock stars.

Having infiltrated the wolves of Wall Street, I knew the only way to survive was to become them. I studied what they talked about, what they valued, how they operated. Every detail was significant. I imitated them with a black StarTAC® cellphone and a new and original device called a BlackBerry®. I also noticed they played a lot of games, unspoken games of hierarchy. Frequent topics of discussions included their homes, their trophy wives, the CEOs they knew, and, of course, the money they were making and spending. The real rainmakers lived in Beverly Hills, Manhattan Beach, Malibu, or Brentwood. If you had a home in one of these zip codes, your stock was the highest. If you didn't have the zip code then you, at the very least, needed to own the latest BMW or Porsche. Riding in these beautiful machines smelled and felt amazing. New leather and 0 to 60 in less than five seconds is something you can't understand just by reading about it, especially for a boy used to riding in a slow, smelly, beat-up Ford van with dusty, stained cloth upholstery. I couldn't help but smile with arrogance when a co-worker would drive us for lunch at Wolfgang's or Crustacean, where the chef would come out to shake our hands and then go to the next table and say hello to a Kurt Russell or a Steven Spielberg.

Bankers and corporate expense accounts are akin to foxes with the keys to the hen house, gorging encouraged. We analysts would compare our Diners Club statements each month. I noticed that the higher the amount, the more important you appeared to the others. My average monthly bill in the first quarter averaged only a couple thousand dollars until the dog learned to travel like a wolf.

You see, I thought the Hilton was an amazing place to stay. Super clean, comfortable, and only $100 to $150 per night. I knew better than to book a beneath-me Holiday Inn. I knew at least I was better than that. But after traveling with a seasoned banker, I quickly learned that the Ritz Carlton, Four Seasons and, if one had to, the W, were a wolf's preferred rental cave. And taxis were for beggars. Private cars and limousines were the only way to travel to the airport and meetings.

Soon I was paying $750 per night at New York's Waldorf Astoria, ordering $500 bottles of wine, receiving $300 massages in my hotel room, and ordering $150 room service for breakfast. Whenever I flew it was first class on American Airlines' red eye from LA to NYC, accruing over 300,000 miles in two years. I would check in to the Waldorf at 7:00 a.m., shower, and check out at 8:00 a.m. That was a $750 one-hour shower.

On one weekend corporate outing, DLJ LA rented out the new Bacara Resort in Santa Barbara, California. Everyone arrived in slick sports cars with their perfectly sculpted Beverly Hills housewives. Free gourmet food, massages, and top shelf booze were complimentary for all. DLJ LA hired an expensive corporate team-building firm based in Los Angeles and they gathered us in a large room for our first activity. The firm had no idea who they were dealing with, no idea what kind of animal it took to survive at DLJ LA. After a couple hours of unsuccessfully trying to get us to participate in their various games, some bankers began to just sit on the ground and not participate, saying that this was stupid and not worth their time. The firm's director saw what was happening, went to the front of the room, and addressed our pack with a microphone. He explained how this would help our office's productivity and allow us to cut down on the hours we were putting in. He totally didn't get us. Boos and laughter from the crowd interrupted him. He was talking and, literally, no one could hear him over the ruckus. Clearly a confident and physically strong man, he looked visibly shaken and then angry while still trying to talk. Then, he went silent and just stared at us. When the booing subsided he ended his contracted weekend prematurely by speaking firmly into the microphone, "In the twenty years I have been doing this kind of work, in building connected teams, I have seen a lot of challenging work environments, but I have never, *ever* witnessed a more dysfunctional, unruly, and unmanageable group of people than I have today." The crowd cheered and the director and his dozens of coordinators left. That's how wolves on Wall Street play; they tear. While I felt bad for the well-intentioned director, this was my pack and neither I nor anyone else stood up to apologize. I looked around and saw mostly conquering smiles and sneers.

With my average Diners Club statements now reaching tens of thousands of dollars per month, I had finally found a family where money was no object and yet the only object. Yeah, this was what I wanted. This is what I dreamed of. This is what I thought would take away the spasms, the sadness, the memory, the shame. And, initially, it did. But the high wore off after the first year of 100-hour workweeks, weekly all-nighters, and unrelenting deadlines. Complain? Not a chance. I worked too hard to get here and there were thousands in Harvard, Berkeley, Stanford, and Wharton who would have killed this dumpster-diving dog for a wolf's ride.

I actually did complain, just secretly in my chest. I wondered how a human being could maintain working 100 hours in seven days, week in and week out. But the wondering and the complaining subsided when my 2001 second-year analyst's W-2 read $212,500, and I knew that in 2002 I would make over $300,000. This trend meant that in 2003 I could break $500,000, and by 2005 I would see an average of $1,000,000 in cash compensation. How did I know this? I asked my VP to show me his paycheck and he did. And then I asked another VP, and she did. I was so close I could taste the freedom I believed a million dollars would bring me. The expected relief in my swelling chest.

*****

Dating your wife while working so many hours requires creativity and flexibility. We met for 1:00 a.m. movies in Century City and 3:30 a.m. dinner at the 24-hour deli. The movies were a bust because I would always fall asleep leaning my head on her shoulder, but I imagine it's all we had space for at the time. We were dating to keep the relationship alive in spite of days without seeing or even talking to one another. There was no time to breathe, let alone sleep, at DLJ LA, only time to work, take speed, and then work some more.

Because I still adhered to my religious rules of not taking drugs or going to strip clubs, my speed was downing cans of Coke for caffeine and my distraction was more work. For many others, it was actual speed or snorting coke to keep them up and running. Some spent long evenings at the Spearmint Rhino, an expensive gentleman's club, as a temporary diversion. Whatever you had to do to stay awake and get that deal closed, to keep you from questioning your career choice, to make that financial model hum, or to hone that presentation to perfection was encouraged.

The level of intense focus and dedication to survive among other wolves sharing similar levels of love for money was beyond human. I amazed myself at how well I could function after skipping a night's sleep and keep blazing through the next day, straight into the next evening—no nap, no shower, and no feelings. Absolutely no genuine feelings were allowed. If I felt fatigue, I had no choice but to pump more caffeine. I could check my financial model for errors for the tenth time. Making a mistake in a model was the quick and unforgiving ticket out of the elite analyst pack. One mistake in one random cell out of the thousands used would push you to the bottom of the respect line—a place that saw no real deal action, just mindless comparable analysis. "An analysis that a trained monkey could do," was how drunk analysts talked about those spreadsheets. We were getting drunk regularly at dinner to give us strength to go back into the office that evening for another 5-6 hour shift. And for those who were the busiest, and therefore, most valued and revered analysts, it was an all-nighter. Sun up to sun up and then another full day until around midnight.

During rare slow periods, in order to save face with the team, some analysts would pretend to work on their PCs. Whenever they heard someone stepping toward them, they quickly switched from Minesweep, Solitaire, or porn to a spreadsheet with a flick of a key stroke. Their animal instincts kept them alert even in the middle of the night, just trying to survive. This behavior was called face time, which no one admitted to doing, but everyone, some more than others, did at some point, especially as bonus time approached.

Bonuses were based on your ranking and determined by the people who had worked with you. Every name was categorized, ranked, and compared. It reminded me of “The Money on the Wall”. Those meetings devolved into shouting matches between associates trying to make sure their star analyst was “taken care of.” They pushed other analysts down in order to elevate their own. Walking by the large conference room could yield great information as to who your allies were and who were wolves in sheep’s clothing. The sound of Wall Street wolves fighting over a finite bucket of bonus money was as ferocious as real wolves fighting over a bone. They were wolves, my wolves, my pack.

At the end of two years, I had been tagged for promotion to Associate, one of only three analysts given this privilege. The other twenty-three analysts had private equity aspirations or were simply not invited to another year’s feast. It was understood that two years was the standard employment time—the length most wolves in previous cohorts had been able to sustain before breaking. I had proven myself worthy, still hungry.

*****

When I first met Amy, I began to have a recurring dream after hearing a popular country song by

Tim McGraw. Like most country songs, *Don't Take the Girl* told a simple, emotional story of two young lovers dealing with difficult scenarios in their lives. The song's second verse finds teenage Johnny and the girl dating and having fallen in love. As Johnny and the girl leave the movie theater on their date they encounter a lone robber. The robber grabs the girl and Johnny tells him he can take everything he has, just not the girl.

In my dream I was Johnny in front of the theater on my knees with my wallet and car keys in my hand begging the robber to take them. I'd wake up in tears, but with a peaceful and relaxed feeling in my chest. It wasn't a nightmare, just my unconscious whispering, revealing my true self to my conscious self.

That dream stuck with me throughout our relationship and later I began to realize how some dreams are poetic in the way they manifest in the "real" world, and some can be eerily prophetic. Amy had just come home from her fourth hospitalization due to mysterious bouts of pancreatitis, and I was working endless hours. She was dealing with loneliness and the potential of an end to her young life, as her Cedars-Sanai doctors could not figure out the cause of her pancreatic attacks. The guilt over being at the office instead of at her bedside began to trigger my back spasms again. I would have to leave in the middle of client meetings and rush to a bathroom stall to grit my teeth through the sudden sharp pains. During this time I was hit with a strong sense of losing the angel in my life. Whether it would be to the pancreatitis or because of the lack of connection that occurs when two people rarely spend time together. I knew we were drifting apart. We needed to spend time together to rekindle our marriage, but the one thing I didn't have at DLJ LA was time. Money, yes, but not time.

In late December 2001, I heard DLJ LA was considering a layoff due to the internet bubble bursting. Within three days of hearing this news, I walked into my managing director's office and drew a graph with time at DLJ on the x-axis and the probability of divorce on the y-axis. I told him that even if the exact percentages were off, the trend was definitely leading toward divorce.

He didn't argue with me; he reached across the table, shook my hand and said, "I really respect your decision." His facial expression told me that he too had seen the trend in investment bankers with ex-wives. The longer you were an investment banker the higher number of divorces you saw. Without thinking, I gave my million dollar aspirations a pause. It was time to move back to Tucson, near family, for support in Amy's recovery.

We had saved enough to qualify for a small mortgage even without having income in Tucson, Arizona. I interviewed at IBM within a week of moving. The hiring manager was a former investment banker and told me he would interview anyone who could get into and survive DLJ LA. Bankers love other bankers almost as much as they love money. I got the offer and started a week later, making a fourth of what I would have made at DLJ LA.

I was twenty-five years old. This move allowed me the experience of choosing something, anything, over money. I never thought I would make such an adverse financial choice, but it felt right, with no hesitation. It felt right in my body. The recurring dream of the robber stopped and even the back spasms subsided, for the time being.

Chapter 8
Fathers Heal

Just before leaving Los Angeles, Amy underwent exploratory surgery, which resulted in removal of her gallbladder and half her pancreas—the part of the pancreas from which her cysts emerged. A biopsy of the cysts revealed precancerous cells. Amy completely recovered in Tucson, and after a time of showing no signs of recurring, we felt it was time to start a family.

Ever since the day my first foster family took me in, I knew I wanted to adopt a child with whom I could share the empathy that came from knowing what it was like to be rejected by birth parents.

IBM's generous flexibility on my work schedule allowed Amy and I to travel to Kazakhstan and meet a fifteen-month-old boy named Akjigit in an orphanage. Akjigit was diagnosed with having a hole in his heart—a common diagnosis in orphans who were available for adoption, a diagnosis that allowed some proud Kazakh people to justify adopting out their orphans to foreigners.

Our first visit to the orphanage was surreal as we toured the facility, seeing the large room with twelve toddler-sized beds, six on each side of the room, all covered by matching brown blankets with smiling turtles and white pillows. Akjigit's birthmother placed him into orphanage care at his birth hospital. No official reason was provided.

Amy and I were given cookies and told to wait in the playroom. Around the corner, we heard the door open and then tiny footsteps. The little boy wobbled at the corner using his bandaged right hand for balance. His caretakers had warned us not to remove the bandage so his raw fingers could heal. Without a mother present, Akjigit had found ways to soothe himself as we all do. He had sucked his right fingers and thumb so often that his hand was covered in open sores due to prolonged exposure to excess moisture. The hair on the back of his head was partially missing because his left hand would rub the same place on his head while he sucked his right hand at night when trying to sleep in a room with eleven other motherless children.

When he peeked around the corner, we formed an immediate bond that was unbreakable, even if a contract were ever to state so. It was a bond that a parent feels when they first see their child, a connection that naturally occurs when a little fifteen-month-old boy hobbles toward you and you give their bandaged hand a cookie.

Time stopped, eyes met, smiles followed, and deep human attachment happened between the three of us. I promised to love and protect this little boy with brown skin, round eyes, chubby cheeks, missing hair, bandaged hand, and hole in his heart.

The experience with my father signing me away had led to this moment, this beautiful moment. And, for the first time since being that fifteen-year-old boy, I felt grateful for the painful experience of rejection, for without it I would not be the lucky father of Sterling Akjigit Smith.

*****

Sometimes life is cloudy; sometimes life is clear. Eighteen months after Sterling joined the Smith family, my twin sons were born and life became very clear. Born nine weeks premature, their 3lb. 6oz. bodies were covered in the fine downy hair that keeps babies warm in the womb until they are able to regulate their own body temperature. Something they were unable to do at thirty-one weeks.

Their delivery was an emergency C-section to save Amy's life from preeclampsia and a ruptured sac. I sat next to Amy, holding her hand, staring into her beautiful blue and green eyes while her doctor pulled out Pierce Aristan Smith and one minute later, Sawyer Mills Smith. Both boys made little sound as their lungs hadn't fully developed.

The nurses let me get close to them for a few minutes, being careful not to get them too close to Amy, as she had contracted pneumonia. If those premature twins had a chance at living, they could not get an infection to add to their struggle. Just before wheeling them away, the nurses raised them high enough for Amy to see over her open belly and hanging placentas. She would be quarantined from them, unable to even be in the same room over the next nine days. She needed to be free from fever before it would be safe for her to touch them. But there was no way of knowing if those babies would still be breathing by then. The most critical moments of their survival would be their first few days, but each day would increase their odds.

Amy is an avid writer, and during this time of separation from her new sons she put what she felt on paper. On Tuesday, April 11, 2006 she wrote:

> *Today is four days after Pierce and Sawyer were delivered and my discharge day. It brings many emotions with it as I am leaving behind my two precious little boys that I know I love but I haven't met*

yet. Yesterday, I spent much of the day in tears, crying over the situation that is ours, yet rejoicing in the little triumphs.

I cried because I am still sick and unable to comfort you and help you through this battle. I cried as I thought of your little three-pound bodies making such strong efforts to survive and thrive in this world you were thrust into. And then I smile when I think, "Survivors and waymakers, this is what is means to be a Smith." You have your daddy who struggled through an impoverished and abusive childhood to become successful in all he sets his mind to. You have me, having battled through health issues and a torn family to be stronger and more committed. There's Sterling, who survived fifteen months in an orphanage until we could be united as a family. And now, there are the two of you, Pierce and Sawyer, the latest additions of Smith survivalists and you are taking on the roles with a sense of entitlement.

I have great faith that you guys will triumph through this and allow yourselves to join this family already a survivor. And then I am reduced to tears again, wishing I could carry all the burdens for you. I look

> *forward to the moment we meet. I look forward to finally touching those thick heads of hair, to taking in your scents, and to being the mother you deserve to have. One day very soon, I promise. Keep fighting!*

As a first-time father to newborns, I was clueless and felt helpless. I stood for hours near their incubators, my hand resting gently on their bodies. The nurses put them together in a single incubator to increase their survival rate. The nurses also recommended I give them something called K-care (short for Kangaroo Care).

On the fourth day, the doctor told us Sawyer was surviving well but Pierce was struggling. Life gets really clear when you hear those words from a doctor about your four-day-old child. Career and wealth, dream homes and cars, extravagant vacations—they all appeared as distant mirages, distractions to what was truly important. I, like my father, begged God to spare my son. I didn't want that lesson. I wasn't going to take that lesson, in this case, standing up.

I was willing to do anything to make sure those boys survived. I became a self-proclaimed K-Care specialist, spending 8-10 hours each day just lying on my back with one or both of my fragile twin boys lying naked on my bare chest, my body heat regulating theirs, my energy helping to circulate theirs. My life's purpose was clear: be completely present for those two, to be there and only there.

IBM was gracious enough to give me the time off without condition to love and K-care my new additions. Though I am grateful it was not an issue, IBM's support wouldn't have mattered in that moment. I was clear and my purpose was to be in that NICU, not the office. My new job was to softly sing to them, tell them how much I loved them and tell them how much fight they had inherited from me. If the latter were even remotely true, these boys were going to make it . . . over my living, breathing, fighting body.

By the time Amy was permitted to hold them, on the ninth day after their birth, their survival was imminent. They had been born having to fight for their lives. They were definitely my sons.

*****

Gibson was two-years-old when his current foster parents, a close family member of Amy's, shared that they would be divorcing. Because their adoption agency was Christian-based, divorce, among other issues, would likely seal the agency's decision to reject the adoption proceedings. We knew this and discussed our options. Our hearts were saying yes to adopting, but we also felt stretched thin with three sons, two of whom had just turned two. To bring in another two-year-old would mean spreading ourselves even thinner, having even less time and energy with each son.

Memories of how I wished for my Mom to spend more time with her fingers in my hair and Amy's concern with her ability to effectively parent four young boys made us pause with the decision. We needed that extra something to know this decision was the right one. We decided to ask Sterling, now 5 ½ years old, how he felt about the possibility of another brother. We wondered what a child might do in this situation.

We painted the landscape for him, including how if we adopted Gibson our time with him and his twin brothers would lessen. This was important as Sterling had been complaining recently about wanting more time with us. After giving Sterling all of the details, he sat on our bed for about two minutes with his eyes closed. We thought he might have gone to sleep, but what he was doing was feeling everything that had been said. His big cheeks were still and then he spoke in the most mature language a five-year-old could muster, "The answer is cwear. Gibson is our famiwy. You adopted me. He needs a famiwy. He would wuv wiving here. We could always use anover brover. Brovers are gweat. We have to adopt Gibson!"

Three months later, Amy received a call from Child Protective Services telling her Gibson was being removed from his foster home and placed in a group home unless we were willing to adopt him. Amy knew our answer but called me anyway for I was on a plane to begin my three-week manager training for IBM in Armonk, New York. When I checked my messages in the lobby of IBM's Learning Center, I recalled my son's lisped clarity. I agreed with Amy that our fourth child, and definitely last, would be another boy.

When Gibson was physically placed in our care, he came with a broken spirit. He didn't play with his new brothers. He just stood in a corner and stared into space. He didn't laugh. He just cried for his mommy. There was no consoling him, no matter what we did. He literally cried himself to sleep for weeks. We felt helpless wishing for his pain to decrease. It simply didn't, no matter what we tried.

About three months after he moved in to his new house, his nightly whimpering still going strong, I remembered the pain I felt at my first foster family's home, those many years ago. I remembered what I wanted in that moment while the shower rained on my broken spirit.

At 10:00 p.m., everyone in bed, I walked into Gibson's room, his tired spirit still whimpering in his half-sleep state. I picked up that little boy, and walked into the back yard, the full moon and the stars reflecting a young man's shadow cradling his new son, my fingers running through his thin, black hair.

The suffering I experienced as a child allowed me to know, from within my chest, what this little boy needed at that moment. To truly know another's pain, one must know their own first. For another moment in my life, I appreciated what I had been through. I was thankful for the pain. Thankful for the loneliness and fear, the hopelessness and rejection, thankful for families who gave to me in my time of need. Now it was my turn to give back. I had endured to give.

In the melody of El Shaddai, (a contemporary Christian hymn my mother sang to me after my time in dark, metal boxes) the cool desert air, the grass, mesquite trees, and saguaros heard a young father softly sing to a broken boy, "Daddy loves Gibson, Gibson loves Mommy, Mommy loves Sterling, Sterling loves Pierce, Pierce loves Sawyer, Sawyer loves Daddy, Daddy loves Gibson, yes he does." I sang softly until his whimpering passed, and only his breath and the dropping of my tears filled the quiet, healing desert.

For many months thereafter I cradled Gibson and any other son who might be having difficulty finding their place in this world or their peace to sleep. The song I first created for Gibson was our anthem—the desert night always listening, listening to a boy held by his father's falling tears of acceptance and gratitude. I was healing my sons which, in turn, was healing me.

SECTION TWO

THE TRUTH SHOP

I could hardly believe my eyes when I saw the name of the shop:
THE TRUTH SHOP.

The saleswoman was very polite: What type of truth did I wish to purchase, partial or whole? The whole truth, of course.
No deceptions for me, no defenses, no rationalizations. I wanted my truth plain and unadulterated. She waved me on to another side of the store.

The salesman there pointed to the price tag.
"The price is very high, sir," he said.
"What is it?" I asked, determined to get the whole truth, no matter what it cost. "Your security, sir," he answered.

I came away with a heavy heart.
I still need the safety of my unquestioned beliefs.

—Anthony de Mello, *The Song of the Bird*, 1982

Chapter 9
Seeker of Truth

Leaving Branhamism after I left my parents' home came fairly naturally. None of the Christian families I lived with followed his teachings, nor had any desire to learn more about a little-known dead prophet. They said Jesus was enough. After some occasional nightmares and panic attacks in my early 20s and some personal due diligence on the "prophecies" Branham had made, I felt safe to leave the prophet and fully attach my eternity to Jesus Christ. Some of my family—those who still believe the "end time message"—were very sad to see me lose my way and blamed my love of money. They said I rejected Branham because I didn't think I needed him anymore. I suppose they were right. They comforted themselves by telling me that God had told them I would come back to the "true message."

As Amy and I were adding sons to our family, my discomfort in teaching them about the path to either heaven or hell also grew. Their innocence was so precious and their trust in what I told them to be true was so freely given.

Like many parents, Amy and I thought it great fun to tell our children about Santa Claus and his magical reindeer. One Christmas Eve we even had their uncle stomp on the roof and yell, "Ho, Ho, Ho!" just as the kids had gone to bed. Wide-eyed, they jumped out of their beds and ran into the living room to find Santa's milk glass empty and only cookie crumbs left on the plate on the fireplace. Some of them excitedly clapped their hands and some cried, probably frightened that someone could enter the house, eat a snack, drop off four new bikes, and climb back up a chimney so quickly. It was beyond their comprehension.

Santa was sown as "fact" into little boys' minds and all it took was any suggestion of its truth because they trusted me. While Santa was not God, something about this still felt too close to home for me. What if my beliefs were also based on such experiences? I was relieved that I only had to do the Santa lie once a year, but I did ponder what other things my children were being taught. I also became concerned for Santa's day of reckoning, the day the boys would eventually find out he wasn't real after all, that I had pretended because, well, that is what normal parents do. But what if, as a result, my sons would also start to doubt their Christian beliefs? I saw danger in this Christmas façade and I also felt doubt creep into my own thoughts, into my own beliefs.

My doubt crystalized when my Christian community vehemently opposed gay partners adopting children. At the time, I also bought into the idea that there was risk that these foster children would have a greater chance of choosing homosexuality if, day after day, they saw a homosexual relationship portrayed as normal and even loving. But, I also believed the risk was worth it considering the alternative for the child, a group home with little individual attention or worse, no home at all.

This was one of the first times my personal beliefs conflicted with my Christian herd and this felt scary to the point that I secretly supported gay couples adopting and simply walked away from these conversations. I felt it was better to keep my dissension to myself as there was a lot to lose in falling out of the good graces of this community.

In early 2008, Oprah and an author I had never heard of before, Eckhart Tolle, were trying out a newer technology called Skype as a way to promote his latest book, A New Earth: Awakening to Your Life's Purpose. Working at IBM, I enjoyed trying new technologies and thought it would be interesting to see how it worked. I began to watch the 10-week series that aired on Monday evenings. The first few weeks kept my attention, primarily because this Tolle character was different looking. He seemed so calm, peaceful, and clear with a strong conviction about "the present moment" and the incessant thoughts that fill the space in our minds. I didn't really see the value in his teaching, as I believed that a constantly running mind was an asset that kept me competitive and successful.

Tolle kept talking about "being without thinking,"—a strange concept to me, but he seemed so certain that incessantly-thinking people were causing themselves and society great unnecessary suffering. While I didn't really understand what he was saying, something kept telling me to keep coming back each week to see what he would say next. I also figured this was a great way to "read" the book without having to buy it.

It was around the fourth or fifth week when Tolle suggested that after the webcast, Skype viewers go into nature and instead of labeling a tree as an oak tree, as a maple tree, or even just as a tree, to just look at it without naming it and just *be* with it. I thought this was a ridiculous exercise, but again his conviction gave me the openness at least to try.

Surrounded by desert, I walked out of our Soldier Trail home onto the trail I had blazed for the kids. I came to a place on the property where I was surrounded by all sorts of barely surviving vegetation. It was April, slightly warm and very dry in the desert. Everything was quiet. Everything was still. A towering, 12-foot saguaro stood in front of me. I stared at it for a long time without labeling it, without describing it, just watching it, and completely focused. All I could feel was my breath.

Then, it happened. The moment that switched on a light within me that could never be turned off. The saguaro appeared to grow larger, both taller and wider, and then began to pulsate, as though it was emanating electric energy. The green colors shimmered into shades I had never before seen. It was as though this inanimate object became alive. I looked around and saw that the whole desert had a similar glowing, fluorescent quality to it. I could feel the desert breathing with me, at the same pace, in the same rhythm. I just stood there laughing and completely enamored at the intense beauty that I sensed had always been there, before my noticing it. I had lived in this type of landscape for over thirty years and had never "seen" it like this before, never experienced its essence like this.

I had no concept of how long I stayed out there that day and had no idea how the experience would begin to affect me. I had experienced a relatively brief moment in time where my mind was not controlling the moment by naming and categorizing the things I had seen. It was a time of no-mind, a time where I felt connected to what I could truly call God without a prophet, without a holy book, without a belief. When I went back into our home office, the sun was setting and things started an unraveling that played out over the next few months.

I began to notice how much my mind labeled everything—a car, a road, the stoplight. I also noticed how my mind was labeling people as Christian, non-Christian, pretty, ugly, old, young, man, woman, on and on. What was strange was that I started to feel connected to everything and everybody. I felt deep compassion for the beggar standing on the island in traffic and I looked him in the face instead of pretending I was busy checking email in my phone.

A pregnant teenager walked by me at a college basketball game and I noticed that I first judged her by thinking she was irresponsible for having a kid so young. And then I just wanted her to have a peaceful pregnancy and for the baby to be loved. Even the outcome of the basketball game became less about who was winning and more about the flow of the passing ball, the momentum of the players, and the energy of the crowd.

At work, I noticed my thoughts when I was with my Hindi coworkers and friends. I thought they were nice and still going to hell. But, they were such nice, peaceful people. Their eternal fate was determined by the country in which they were born. This seemed unfair that I had a greater opportunity for eternal salvation while my unlucky Hindi friends were likely going to be in eternal agony after this relatively very short life. The thoughts were disturbing and I realized had always been there. I was just used to having my judging mind do its thing, unchecked, unnoticed, unquestioned. I shared this with the psychiatrist I had been seeing regularly for the last two years, and he seemed intrigued too. He asked me if I had taken any drugs in addition to the one for my ADHD. I had not.

As I became more aware of my religious beliefs, more aware of the thinking around them, the more I wondered if they were true, really true, or just a Santa story that I had been taught.

My intellect became thirsty for books written by non-Christians and I couldn't believe what I was reading. There were so many books that viewed God as more of a created idea than a real entity. Robert Wright's Evolution of God walked me through the history of the concept of god in the Abrahamic religions and how the concept of god changed in a particular society as the society's needs changed. For instance, when a society wanted to do business or co-exist with another society, each society's god seemed to be more tolerant and accepting of the other. However, when a society was oppressed or enslaved by another group, then their god's views would become more belligerent and intolerant. Same god, just with extreme mood changes, less god and more human.

Through reading books I was discouraged by my church to read, the scariest of questions arose, "What if I was wrong? What if I had helped bring people to Jesus without a full understanding of Christianity? What if teaching my children that fearing God was the highest form of love, was not love at all, but simply control? What if I was just like my father?"

These questions would surface for a while and then I would get busy with work and the questions seemed to dissipate until the next lull in life. Everything came to a head on Easter 2009 as I was singing in church that my God was an awesome God, that He poured down judgment and wrath on Sodom, and that He was an awesome God. While I read the words on the giant screen above the pulpit, I realized I wasn't singing anymore. I was just standing there in a church with hundreds of people singing and I was the only one silent. I couldn't sing the words if I didn't believe my God was awesome for burning down an entire city for not following His rules.

After church, I went to a family barbeque. Instead of socializing, I locked myself in a room and continued my research on the validity of the Bible, particularly on the resurrection of Jesus. I reasoned that what made Christianity better than other religions was the "fact" that its leader had risen from death. Therefore, I reasoned that if the resurrection did not happen, then the whole story was just that, a story, and at least some parts were not to be taken literally. Without the resurrection, which is why Easter was deemed as being even more important to Christianity than Christmas, then Christianity was just like any other religion. Not special as I was taught, and I was not special as I was taught for believing it.

After five hours, the barbeque was over and I got into the car with the family. Amy was angry that I had vanished for the whole day without warning. I answered her with, "I was doing some research that couldn't wait."

"Research on what?"

"The resurrection."

Amy's eyes widened. I hadn't shared my doubts with her.

"Amy, I don't think Jesus literally rose from the dead."

Nothing else was said on the way home. It was a blow to both of us. We had made God the center of our relationship, our entire life, and I had just crossed a line that was unfathomable and unforgivable.

After a few days of shock and loud conversations, Amy told me that I needed to move out until I figured out my truth. I refused and then she began packing her and the kids' suitcases to move out of Soldier Trail. I told her that she was going too far and that I just needed more time to work it out. She fell on the bed and wept.

During the next couple of months, hours and hours of heated and sobering conversations occurred. She was hurt that I had kept my doubts secret from her. I told her that I was afraid to even acknowledge them to myself.

Through much patience and honest listening, Amy tempered her threats to leave with the kids and began her own inquiry. The few Christian friends she did tell about my blasphemy advised her to leave me. Amy's honest inquiry allowed for both of us, together and separately, in our own time and pace, to research and question.

I held on to my learned Christian beliefs a little longer than Amy and gave one last attempt to turn back to God. In a coming out letter to my Facebook friends, mostly Christians, I explained I was experiencing deep doubts in the validity of my faith. I asked for honest dialogue and a safe place where I could voice the concerns I had. In the beginning, the dialogue was respectful but at many times empty. I was told every Christian goes through these bouts with doubt and that I would surely find my faith to be even stronger when I came out on the other side. My extracurricular reading told me the same thing and that there were also people who had left their faith forever.

As goes most social media conversations, discourse turned to debate and then to personal attacks. One Facebook friend said she was so sad for our children, who now were never going to experience love, God's love. She felt sorry for how our innocent kids would be impacted by the choices their parents were making. She didn't understand why we reacted with an angry comment by defending that we still planned to love our children, with or without God. Some blamed my deceased father's rigid and abusive behavior for my retaliation against God. Some friends warned me that I was inviting God's wrath by questioning His goodness. Other friends said they were just going to pray for me.

I certainly was not always respectful with my comments either. I accused people of not being completely honest with their own doubt and personal moral convictions. I also accused parents of using fear to control their children's beliefs in their God. At times, I noticed I tried to win the conversation rather than acknowledge a valid argument. As grief set in, my anger was directed toward people I once called community.

Some of my community began to unfriend me on Facebook, particularly my former high school educators, who I admonished for their emphasizing the "evidence" that demanded clear support of the Bible and never mentioning the overwhelming facts that proved the Bible could not possibly be a literal interpretation of history. I felt duped and angry, and I wanted revenge, to have others feel the pain I was feeling.

Some cut off communication and others paid visits to our living room for one last plea. My former high school baseball coach, a confident, funny man, spent an evening with me reminiscing over my first home run and how he loved coaching me. The last couple of hours of our conversation ended with an emotional plea using Pascal's Wager, a form of insurance against hell. Briefly, Pascal's Wager posits that humans all bet with their lives either that God exists or not. Given the possibility that God actually does exist and assuming an infinite gain or loss associated with belief or unbelief in said God (as represented by an eternity in heaven or hell), a rational person should live as though God exists and seek to believe in God. If God does not actually exist, such a person will have only a finite loss (some pleasures, luxury, etc.).[2]

The underlying problem I told him was that while I certainly wanted an insurance policy from hell, as I had demonstrated at my baptism before the age of seven, I couldn't fool an omnipotent being, one that could read my mind and know that I was truly not a believer or even a supporter of some Christian doctrines. I told him there was no hiding from God and, truly, I was tired of worshipping anything out of fear. He and I, ironically the 1995 Christian Student Athlete of the Year, hugged and said goodbye.

The final Facebook nail in my Christian coffin came when the question was asked if we had to choose between being a "Seeker of Truth" or "Defender of the Faith," which would we choose. A Christian friend, who frequently participated in these debates, unconvincingly argued these choices were indeed the same, but upon pressing him to choose one he proudly chose to be a "Defender of the Faith."

The trial had run its course. As more and more time on Facebook produced less and less reason to continue the grieving process online, I deactivated my account, left a belief system I had thought was truer than anything I had ever known, and became a Seeker of Truth.

Chapter 10
Million Dollar Cup of Water

Some have joked that IBM must stand for "I've Been Moved," as it is customary for high potential employees to move every 18-24 months. IBM develops its leaders by placing them in challenging positions and after achieving mastery of the assigned role, they are then reassigned to the next challenge, and the next, and so on. Meet any IBM executive and simply ask them where they've lived and you'll have them talking about the expats in Malaysia, how much money they saved in Singapore due to the US dollar's strength, or the help they were able to hire in India. An adventurous life indeed but not ideal with a wife and four sons now ages 6, 3, 3, and 3.

I opted to stay in Tucson for as long as I could, hoping my career would not suffer while I enjoyed the company of my young family. Potty training three three-year-olds was especially memorable as we discovered that just letting them go outside in the backyard was more effective than bribing them with cookies. Life was simple as sons and father crossed their streams with their big boy smiles, ending with sometimes wet, high fives. But I knew such simple times were only temporary as my desire to be more and make more grew and my career at IBM stopped moving up when I declined for the fourth time to move to headquarters in Armonk, New York. It was time to look for a company in Tucson where we could continue to rear these precious boys surrounded by family and friends.

As chance would have it, I was not the only IBMer who chose home over career. A former manager of mine in IBM's Pricing and Investment Analysis group had left a couple of years prior to work for Roger Vogel, the CEO of Vante, a former plant manager for the IBM Tucson site where 2,000 people had been employed under his leadership. Vante, a place for former IBMers to stay and play in Tucson, was in need of a CFO. My former manager vouched for me and I started with Vante in February 2010.

Vante was a medical device manufacturer, had been around for thirty years, and had about 100 employees. Many of those employees had been with the company for a decade or two. Roger had just sold one of two divisions of the business to a public company and as a result forty employees either had been transferred to the public company or simply laid off.

On my first day, I was introduced to most of the employees in groups of ten in the conference room. Their energy was sad, broken, and scared.

They had worked with some of those forty employees for their entire professional careers. They were a family torn apart to make room for a more profitable business. While I knew I was hired for my finance and accounting skills, my heart was pulled to create an environment that felt safe, fun, and purposeful. They needed this and I felt compelled to create a place where current employees' resumes weren't so pervasive on resume.com, where meetings didn't feel like funerals, and where leaders led with their hearts and not just their profit and loss statements.

Once I became settled in the CFO role, I began to meet with employees during their breaks, lunches, and after work. I wanted to know what they needed to make Vante a place where people loved to work, felt purpose in their daily tasks, and overall, just felt cared for. Initially, the employees were skeptical and distrusting of my IBM background, assuming I was just another big company man seeing them as resources instead of humans, instead of the little children we all are at the core. Love, transparency, authenticity, and deep listening cuts through fear and distrust. This is the lesson I witnessed in my interactions with the assemblers, engineers, receptionists, sales people, and support staff. People let down their guard, warmed up, began to voice their concerns, and began to trust that I meant what I was saying and doing. I too was feeling a deeper connection to my extended leadership role and with the people I began to view as my extended family.

In 2011 the Vante family was healing. The cafeteria was re-painted to resemble a warm, inviting French café. We installed a foosball table, 50” television, and subsidized snack and soda machines. A dartboard was hung in the engineers’ work space. A basketball hoop was set up in the parking lot. And a small gym was added to the basement with a bench press, stationary bike, treadmill, punching bag, and another 50” television. We were a 60-employee company acting like a mini-Google. It was so rewarding to see the diverse little company come together for BBQs on the patio complete with adult beverages. People were smiling and talking again and I just loved watching it all unfold.

We had fun, but we also cared. One of my employees came in to work one day visibly upset. That morning as she walked with her two young kids to her car parked on the street outside her home, she saw broken glass in the driver’s seat and noticed her red iPod had been taken from the console. She was able to distract her kids long enough to pick up the glass, roll down the other windows to match the broken window, and turn on the heater to counter the morning's cold in an effort to protect them from feeling scared and unsafe. As she drove them to school and daycare, her daughter asked why they weren't listening to music and singing on the way, as this was their routine. She told her daughter the iPod must have been left in the house. Now, this mother was shaking in front of me, worried about the window, how the kids might react when they found out how their family morning routine had been stolen and that their space had been violated. I had plenty of "to dos" that day planned for my team and me, but a new task shot to the top of that list. An hour later, I called the mother into my office to see how she was doing and to give her a small gift from Costco. When she opened the small box, she put her hands over her face and began to cry as she sat in the chair across my desk. The note on the box read, "So the kids can hear their morning music with Mom. We, here at Vante, care about our family." A new iPod, the same color as the one stolen that morning, lay in her lap. To see such a deep longing within her to just keep her kids' lives stable and safe brought tears. We cried and hugged like longtime friends.

When she left my office, I closed my door, put my head on my desk and felt the love that extended past traditional familial ties and quashed corporate coldness. I was hired to count Vante's money, but I was even more inspired to keep leading with love.

*****

On August 1, 2012, my iPhone chimed and a reminder popped up, "Protest Chick-fil-A® Appreciation Day." This protest originated in response to Chick-Fil-A Appreciation Day, a day created by Fox News host, former Arkansas governor, and ordained Southern Baptist minister, Mike Huckabee. The purpose of this event was to support Chick-Fil-A President and COO Dan Cathy, who had been making media waves in July 2012 when he said the company was "Guilty as charged" and "very much supportive of the family—the biblical definition of the family unit. We are a family-owned business, a family-led business, and we are married to our first wives. We give God thanks for that."[3] In a separate interview Cathy stated, "as it relates to society in general, I think we are inviting God's judgment on our nation when we shake our fist at Him and say 'we know better than you as to what constitutes a marriage' and I pray God's mercy on our generation that has such a prideful, arrogant attitude to think that we have the audacity to try to redefine what marriage is all about."[4] It was documented that Chick-Fil-A had donated millions of dollars to anti-gay groups such as the Marriage & Family Foundation, Fellowship of Christian Athletes, Exodus International and the Family Research Council—some of which supported "reparative therapy" for homosexuals (which seeks to turn gays and lesbians into heterosexuals) and that pedophilia was a "homosexual problem." The YouTube protest I planned to participate in was initiated by a YouTube vlogger, Jackson Pearce, who encouraged people to order a free cup of water on Chick-Fil-A Appreciation Day, videotape oneself doing so, and send her the video where she would include it as a response to her video. Her video can still be found on her channel at: https://www.youtube.com/watch?v=JprRWKQys7A .

There was a Chick-fil-A store on my way to the office. As I drove by, I noticed the long line that had already snaked around the mall parking lot. The line was too long to participate and still make my usual 8:00 a.m. start time. I consciously made the choice to focus on my career rather than social change. It was a familiar choice to me. One that had taken me from a double-wide with exposed white, plastic piping in the far outskirts of the Tucson desert to now living in my newly renovated, adobe dream home with a three-car garage, Vega beam ceilings, stainless steel kitchen, new covered decks, and salt water pool and spa, surrounded by scores of towering saguaros and giant mesquite and palo verde trees, all on 3.3 acres bordered by 6.7 acres of undeveloped land, at the base of majestic Mount Lemmon. This was my improved version of the ten acres on which I grew up—my "virtually impossible" version of ten acres that was gained by being money focused.

The protest seemed simple; yet, within me, I could feel bubbling to the surface the teachings of my formative years that gays were evil and, therefore, should not be allowed to marry, to adopt, and didn't even deserve to be treated equally. My courage felt small and insignificant in the shadow of my hate training. I had grown up as a fundamentalist Christian, following the teachings of a prophet. Here I was, now questioning everything and lovingly encouraging the same of my boys. This simple YouTube counter protest to Chick-fil-A's Appreciation Day seemed like a safe and harmless way for me to finally use a voice I had not heard or been allowed to share: my voice. I set another reminder to use my lunch break as a time to protest by ordering a free cup of water and telling Chick-Fil-A that not everyone appreciated their funding of anti-gay organizations.

At lunch my back began to give me the early warnings of another spasm coming on. I was now trained to know that when this happened, there was an underlying message my body was sending me. Maybe it was having mindlessly skipped my daily ADHD meds. Maybe it was skipping my daily bike ride. Maybe it was the confrontation I had with executives the prior afternoon regarding my repeated and continuing accounting concerns that the team felt pressured to ignore in order to make our year-end September bonuses. Maybe it was something I was unaware of, something deeper that calls us to places we would not go if we knew what lie ahead. But I could feel it in my body and I was tired of feeling any more pain, tired of gay human beings being the brunt of public jokes, harassment, and ridicule. I was tired of the hate.

My phone chimed again. Time to protest. Time to take my first public stand for equality. While waiting in the drive-thru line, I felt alone, secretly hoping the other cars in line were also ordering free cups of water in protest. I listened to the orders of the two cars in front of me. Orders of food and soda. No free cups of water for them. I was doing this alone, on my personal time, without the protection of a herd or pack. The energy of justice triggered adrenaline as I ordered my free cup of water and slowly approached the drive-thru window with my iPhone recording the two and one-half minutes that would change my life forever.

From what I know of that day, the young lady (Rachel) working the drive-thru was a shift leader recently trained for the possibilities of protesters on this appreciation day. My free cup of water order certainly would've sounded peculiar. Regardless of any chest tightening or other warning signals firing off inside of me, regardless of the human being on the other side of my iPhone recording, I had something to voice and that became of utmost importance. When I approached the window I greeted Rachel and the following conversation ensued:

Adam Smith: Hey, how you doing?

Rachel: Fine.

Adam Smith: Good. Is this my free water?

Rachel: It is.

Adam Smith: Awesome. You know why I'm getting the free water, right?

Rachel: I do not.

Adam Smith: Cause Chick-Fil-A is a hateful corporation.

Rachel: I disagree . . . I wouldn't . . . I . . .

Adam Smith: I know but . . .

Rachel: We don't treat any of our customers

differently; we don't discriminate for hiring practices.

Adam Smith: I know, but you . . . the corporation gives money to hate . . . to hate groups. Hate groups. Just because people wanna kiss another guy.

Rachel: I'm . . . I'm staying neutral on this subject. I have to stay neutral on this subject. My personal beliefs should not be at the workplace.

Adam Smith: I believe that too.

Rachel: Yeah

Adam Smith: I don't believe corporations should be giving money to hateful groups.

Rachel: I'm really uncomfortable that you're videotaping me right now.

Adam Smith: Totally understand . . .

Rachel: Ok

Adam Smith: . . . I'll take my water.

Rachel: It's my pleasure to serve you always.

Adam Smith: Oh yeah, of course, I'm glad that I can take a little bit of money from Chick-Fil-A and maybe less money to hate groups.

Rachel: Well, well we're always . . .

Adam Smith: Have a good day.

Rachel: We're happy to serve every – all of our guests.

Adam Smith: I don't know how you live with yourself and work here. I don't understand it. This is a horrible corporation with horrible values.

Rachel: We are here to serve you in any way that you need.

Adam Smith: You deserve better.

Adam Smith: Rachel, you deserve better. Okay?

Rachel: I hope you have a really nice day.

Adam Smith: I will; I just did something really good, I feel purposeful, thank you so much.

Rachel: Have a good day.

Adam Smith: Okay, I'm a nice guy by the way and I'm totally heterosexual.

Rachel: You are really nice.

Adam Smith: I have not a gay in me, I just can't stand the hate, you know. It gotta stop. It's gotta stop guys. Stand up.

Rachel: Okay, have a nice day sir.

Adam Smith: All right, see ya, guys.

I felt conflicted inside and, before forwarding the protest to the YouTube organizer, I sent the video to my non-confrontationally-inclined wife. She watched and texted back "That was rough to watch." I agreed and decided to apologize to Rachel when the long lines and crowds had subsided. I also assumed the video would be edited by the YouTube protest organizer before being publicly posted on her YouTube channel. To send the video to the protest organizer, I had to upload the video to my personal YouTube account and then forward it to the organizer. I pressed upload and went back to work to deal with the current accounting challenges.

That evening was like any other: dinner with the family, tucking in the boys, sharing a glass of wine with my wife and friends, conversation by an outdoor fire, and occasionally checking email. One work email caught my attention. It was from someone outside my contact list and essentially said, "We know who you are. We have contracted with a face recognition software company to certify that you are the vile executive that attacked the helpless CFA drive-thru operator today. We have certified the face in the YouTube video with your LinkedIn account. We now have your personal and work information and will be contacting your CEO, Board of Directors, and your customers to show what a despicable thing you did. We will not stop until you have paid for what you have done."

Moments later my cell phone began to receive scores of calls from area codes primarily in Oklahoma. Some left text messages. Some left voicemails. All left messages of hate or threats. Threatening messages detailing the ways in which I was going to pay.

Personally, I thought these messages to be over-reactive, but I wanted to ensure my company was prepared for what may be happening so I sent the email and video to a fellow Vante executive and called for his advice. He watched it and told me the video was harmless and respectful for a protest and that I had nothing to worry about. He said he would increase security on our servers just in case. I went to delete the video from my YouTube account, not from fear of retribution but because my intent was never to propel myself or Rachel into the spotlight of this heated Chick-fil-A debate. Access to my account had somehow had been blocked and I was unable to delete the video. And now hundreds of emails began to stream in to my inbox.

I turned my busy iPhone off, slept fairly soundly, and had faith that all would be clear and calm in the morning. On my bike ride into the office the next morning, I stopped by the same Chick-fil-A store to apologize to Rachel. Not having a bike lock and now with the drive-thru lane completely clear of any supporters or dissenters, I biked up to the drive-thru window and asked to speak to Rachel. I was told she did not want to talk with me. I understood and asked the messenger to please tell her I was sorry for how I protested and how I spoke to her. As I cycled off, I noticed a phone staring back at me. Later, I would find out that this was Rachel's fiancé filming me.

A few minutes later, I walked into the familiar doors of Vante and said hello to the front desk receptionist. Her eyes were wide and in shock. She asked me, “Adam, what did you do?!?” I thought there was no way she could have been privy to what had happened. But, she had come into the office earlier that morning and had checked phone messages. She told me the voicemail was filled to capacity and horrible threats had been made to the company.

I went to my office, dropped off my bike, and went to find an executive who would be able to fill me in. I was met with concerned faces and strict instructions to go into my office and say nothing to anyone. There had been bomb threats made and those threats required Vante to have every employee go home for the day. In fact, Vante would shut its doors for the two remaining days of the workweek due to the threats. I checked my email and saw myself CC’d on derogatory and inflammatory emails sent to my CEO, Board of Directors, and other Vante employees. We were being cyber-bullied, attacked by someone with no physical body but a powerful manipulator of fear. I felt angry that people would attack my extended corporate family for a personal stand of mine.

I suggested to the other executives that I publicly apologize and provide context as to what

I was doing. The suggestion was immediately shut down and I was told to leave the office out of safety. I was told to remain radio silent.

I rode home confused and dizzy, wondering if I would soon wake up from this surreal and chaotic moment. I arrived home around noon and told Amy what had happened at Vante. I went outside and sat at the edge of my driveway to breathe and to find some grounding in the magnificent and familiar sight of Mount Lemmon. Amy sat in silence beside me.

Around 12:30 p.m. the University of Arizona called me informing me that they too had received threatening calls and demands that I be fired. I had taught a business course in their MBA program earlier that year and had verbally agreed to teach an executive course for them during the fall. They asked what Vante was doing in response to the events. I had no answers.

And then I received a call from Vante's CEO. His voice was quivering. He asked no questions. He simply told me he needed me to resign. No room for my side of the story. I told him that I disagreed with his decision and that these attacks were from bullies. I said he was overreaching and that he shouldn't punish me over a personal stand I took on my personal time. The CEO said that if I refused to resign he would need to fire me. I did not resign. He said I left him no choice, "Adam, you are fired."

I did not know that he planned to issue a press release. I suppose it was to more easily communicate to the bullies that they should stop harassing Vante. Regardless, when the formal statement was sent in the form of a press release, every media outlet in the world also received the same statement:

> *Vante regrets the unfortunate events that transpired yesterday in Tucson between our former CFO/Treasurer Adam Smith and an employee at Chick-fil-A. Effective immediately, Mr. Smith is no longer an employee of our company.*
>
> *The actions of Mr. Smith do not reflect our corporate values in any manner. Vante is an equal opportunity company with a diverse workforce, which holds diverse opinions. We respect the right of our employees and all Americans to hold and express their personal opinions, however, we also expect our company officers to behave in a manner commensurate with their position and in a respectful fashion that conveys these values of civility with others.*

> *We hope that the general population does not hold Mr. Smith's actions against Vante and its employees.*[5]

After Vante's release, the University of Arizona quickly followed up with their own:

> *Adam Smith held an appointment as an Adjunct Lecturer, Finance (non-tenure eligible) in the Eller College of Management at the University of Arizona from January 2, 2012, to May 20, 2012. He presently holds no appointment with the University.*
>
> *The University of Arizona is committed to being a community in which all members support the free and respectful exchange of varied ideas and perspectives. We strive to have a workforce that is diverse and respectful of different viewpoints.*[6]

The University of Arizona followed up with a call to tell me they no longer needed me to teach the executive MBA course for the next semester, and then they removed my teaching profile from their website.

Over the course of my two-and-a-half years there, Vante had awarded me equity in the form of restricted stock. The only restriction on the stock was that I had to be employed in order to sell the stock when the company was either sold or raised money for expansion, which we were working on at the time of the protest. As a result of my firing that equity was revoked.

In one day, with one two-and-one-half minute YouTube video protest, my salary and equity vanished. The security I believed would keep me safe from chance, bad luck, bad people, Satan, and fire forever had been taken. More than one million dollars of value was gone in an instant. That free cup of water ironically cost me a million dollars.

Chapter 11
More to Pay

I imagine Vante and The University of Arizona quickly cut their ties to me in order to silence the bullies infiltrating their emails and voicemail boxes. The bullies may have stopped their war against my former employers but they had just begun their attack against me. While my entire net worth, except for the $100,000 we had saved for retirement, had completely vanished, I still had more to pay.

I had been fired from two employers in a matter of hours and began to wonder if I should take the cyber threats seriously as well. My YouTube account became accessible again and I promptly removed the protest video. At that point, the video had a measly amount of hits. Maybe 600.

And then my wake-up call came. A friend's caller ID showed up on my phone. I answered. He told me I needed to turn on the television and tune in to Fox News. Fox had been running constant coverage of the success of Governor Huckabee's Chick-fil-A Appreciation Day. I expected to see more of the same as I switched on the network. Instead, I stood stunned, my chest tightening, angst running through my veins. The YouTube video that I had recently removed was playing on Fox News. Vante's press release had not only alerted the cyber bullies of my consequence but also every news organization in the world. Fox News ran the story, "Viral Video of Man Picking on Chick-fil-A Worker Gets Him Fired."[7]

Besides the missing facts that I was protesting and that the company was receiving bomb threats, I didn't think 600 views warranted the term "viral," so I looked on YouTube just to make sure I had removed the video. The video had been removed but I learned that a video can be "mirrored" or copied and simply reposted by other YouTube channel operators—a common practice where the operators also add advertisements at the beginning of the video and then profit a couple cents per view. Their total views were approaching 100,000 hits, which meant that the video, if it hadn't technically done so already, was indeed about to go viral and all I could do was watch it unfold.[8]

Phone calls continued to flood in. Angry phone calls. Threatening calls. Concerned calls. Media calls. Calls from friends filling me in on the madness rampantly spreading across media forums. One friend found my personal cell and email address posted on several sites encouraging viewers to contact and harass me. Another friend alerted me to a false Facebook page. I had closed my Facebook account approximately a year prior to this event so I was surprised to see a new Facebook page with pictures of me and posts simulated to appear as though I had written them. Pictures of me and my family were visible on this page with posts that read, “Hello, my name is Adam Smith. I berate drive-thru employees,” “I am interested in men and children”, “I believe pedophiles like me should be free to ‘play’ with children unattended.” Pictures of my children and links to pornographic sites, were included on this pseudo Facebook page. I immediately contacted Facebook to begin the process of removing the page. There are no words to explain the pain one feels when their innocent little boys are being used as props in a war waged by unscrupulous adults.

Personal bank statements soon surfaced online. One “news” article written for *The Telegraph* titled, “Is Adam M Smith, the Chick-fil-A hater and America’s rudest liberal, an Obama donor?” accused me of using Vante’s funds to make a donation to the Obama campaign. My now ex-Director of HR brought this article to my attention. After a long, uncomfortable pause, I sensed she needed evidence that the “news” article was inaccurate. I sent my former HR department a copy of my personal credit card statement. Proof that I had made a singular $250 donation to the

Obama campaign with my personal credit card. Hardly the extreme left campaign donor sold as news, but I thought it was strange that Vante was questioning my character *after* firing me.

There was a moment I will never forget when a family member showed me a post in which someone had accurately shared my home address and the address to the elementary school my children attended. The post encouraged everyone in the Tucson area to drive by my kid's school and harass my sons in their third grade and kindergarten classrooms.[9] I could handle the smears, the sensationalism, the false accusations, and thousands of comments being spread by the media. What I could not handle were the threats against my family.

At that moment, everything that seemed important in terms of losing my job and reputation became totally and completely irrelevant and insignificant. My instinct to protect my children kicked in and that became my focus. We were being hunted by invisible predators with the ability to activate thousands with just a few key strokes. We were fully exposed, completely vulnerable, surrounded by threats, and some of them very violent in nature. Per the advice of our local police department, we immediately found a hotel room, paid in cash, and turned off location sharing on our phones.

On the third day, the hunting continued. Amy and I went by the house to grab the boys' inhalers and medications, as well as personal necessities needed while we were away from our home. The plan was for the grandparents to house the boys to keep them sheltered from this mess and Amy and I would stay with her sister. We arrived home to find handwritten notes nailed to the front door. None of them filled with pleasantries. I opened the mailbox and found letters, some postmarked and some not. Amy opened one package that looked like something she must've ordered online only to find a sealed bag of what, at first glance, looked like mud. Amy kneeled down on the driveway, her face in her hands, and began to sob. Someone had taken time and spent money to have feces mailed to us. It was difficult to have so much hate being channeled toward me.

Hundreds of hate-filled emails continued to pour in. I sifted through them hoping for any that were positive or offered a bit of hope in this chaotic and dark time. There were only a few and most of them said that what had happened was a direct call from God to get my attention and turn to follow Him.

One email had a subject line that read, "Good afternoon, from Fox News." I opened it and the email was from a .foxnews email address, which was followed up with a phone call requesting an interview with Bill O'Reilly. Similar emails and calls came in from CNN, *USA Today*, the *Wall Street Journal*, etc., all requesting interviews regarding my reactions to headlines like, "CFO Attacks Chick-fil-A Woman." I was more concerned with keeping my boys' asthma, anxiety, and other special needs cared for. I was more concerned with shielding them from the disaster that was re-shaping our future. I was doing everything in my power to keep calm, collected, and focused on what my family needed to remain safe and cared for. I was more focused on those matters than on commenting publicly on sensationalized "facts." Besides, the public had already formed their opinion. At this point, anything I said would likely only cause more damage.

That third evening, when the kids were at an address that had not been publicly placed on the Internet, I felt space to record an unedited video, the video I wanted to make while at Vante to communicate the context and apologize for the way I spoke to Rachel. This apology video received far less YouTube views than the protest video.[10]

The O'Reilly Factor ran the fired executive

story three times during the first two weeks.[11] My story played out like a fictional movie right in front me. The third story he ran involved a body language expert named Tonya Reiman to determine whether or not the apology video I had made was authentic. O'Reilly first had the expert analyze a video of President Obama in a room full of senators. Obama had his finger over his mouth while listening to Republican Paul Ryan speak. This was interpreted by the body language expert as Obama needing to say something but being willing to wait for the senator to finish speaking. The expert deemed both Ryan and Obama were being respectful and courteous in their interactions and taking personal responsibility for what they were saying.

Next, O'Reilly played a video of Secretary of State Hillary Clinton dancing with women in South Africa. Reiman pointed out that Hillary looked uninhibited, that she was truly having fun dancing and was not performing for the camera. She was deemed genuine.

Then O'Reilly played snippets of my apology video to Rachel as the body language expert watched:

Adam Smith: Rachel, I am so very sorry for the way I spoke to you on Wednesday. You handled my frustrating rant with such dignity and composure.

Every time I watch the video I am blown away by really the beauty in what you did and your kindness and your patience with me.

Bill O'Reilly: All right, acting job or sincere?

How could this body language expert on the right-leaning Fox News find the two most high-profile Democrats genuine and then be analyzing an apology video of a fired CFO of a small 60-employee company? It was both surreal and disturbing to see how the media inflated me into a bigger persona than I was. The body language expert answered:
Tonya Reiman: Sincere. Three quick things. The first is he is looking all around, trying to replay what he did in his head. The second thing is he is speaking in very clip tones, which tells me he is embarrassed for what he did. And, the third thing is as he is trying to come up with an answer he says, "beauty, kindness, and patience," and he tilts his head to the side exposing his own vulnerability. So, I think this was genuine.

Bill O'Reilly: Couldn't you fake that though?

O'Reilly pushing back on the analyzer in his typical powerful and persuasive tone, caused my breath to stop, wondering if Reiman would buckle under the pressure. I was a nobody. I didn't have political clout that might protect me from a third party assessment of authenticity. I was just a "liberal bully" who got what he deserved. And while I knew my apology was genuine, I also knew that perception was reality and she held the reality of the millions of viewers who made The O'Reilly Factor the most watched cable news program in the United States. She answered Bill with a firm and clear analysis:

Tonya Reiman: You could, but you know what, it wouldn't match. The voice and the movements would not match and here they match.

Bill's face softened.

Bill O'Reilly: You thought that was natural?

Tonya Reiman: Yes, I did think that it was natural.

Bill O'Reilly: Well, I'm going to give him the benefit of the doubt too.

He then asked someone off stage if I had received my job back.

Bill O'Reilly: Did he get his job back because I said over the air earlier that I thought he should get his job back and I hope he did.

Through his earpiece he was told that I had not. He looked disappointed.

Bill O'Reilly: He did not get his job back? Well, I hope someone in Arizona hires the guy. I hope they do.[12]

Hearing these words from one of the most energetically charged and conservative talking heads in the media gave me hope that this whole fiasco would come to an end as quickly as it had begun. I had hope that I would be providing for my family once again. Maybe our much-needed health insurance would not lapse after all. I breathed in hope and quietly thanked Bill for the unintended but encouraging words.

The YouTube protest video now showed a view count of over one million hits with vicious comments that felt like one million gut punches. Articles emerged from all over the world, most of them affirming that I had received what I deserved. I started to believe it as well. Perhaps this was fair and just. Maybe I deserved all of the consequences. I wondered if I was the wretched, abusive, out-of-control person they said I was. A majority of the comments written in response to these articles agreed that I was punished fairly or was still in need of even harsher punishments, including death and the removal of my kids.

I made some initial inquiries into getting another executive role in Tucson, but after speaking with recruiters it was clear that Tucson's executive job market wasn't ready to have me. Recruiters advised I try again in six months when the name "Adam Smith" was not associated with such negative publicity. A public relations specialist advised me to remain quiet and let this all blow over. Our financial needs could not wait six months. We had saved for retirement, but everything else had been contractually taken by Vante when they fired me. With little chance of income for six months in Tucson and no ability to pay the $3,333 interest-only mortgage of our home and a necessary Cobra insurance payment of $1,200, Amy and I laid in bed holding each other as we discussed our limited options.

We realized we needed to accept the events taking place. There was no denying their existence. To resist them would be to our demise. We needed truth and clarity to allow space for a new beginning. The truth was that we were jobless, unemployable, without a safe home, smeared, and broken. We laid in bed reminiscing our eighteen years together. We shared memories of our life adventures, enjoying the days past. We stayed up all night, snuggled together talking and comforting. Amy calls it one of the best nights of her life and I would agree. It is a night I will remember always. It was the night where two childhood friends became adult friends, a night where two people met in acknowledgement of the other's importance in their life. We laughed at the absurd reality we witnessed those past two weeks. We mourned the loss of a comfortable and predictable life. We had lived and loved and now change was at our door screaming that it was time for a new chapter in this story of ours.

We felt the movement of this change and began to make arrangements to leave the home we had designed specifically for our testosterone-energized family—the home we thought would be the place where we would grow old, where we would play with our grandchildren. We also felt the need to purge the experience and start over. By the end of August, just a few weeks after the Chick-fil-A incident, we had sold or donated everything we could not fit into the old RV we had just purchased from Craigslist for $5,000. Televisions, couches, tables, beds, everything gone. The four boys, Amy, and I said goodbye to the grave of our dog Shadow that rested in the dry wash running through our property. We said goodbye to the newly remodeled kitchen and bathrooms, to the exotic wood floors, the pool and spa, the bike trail, and the wraparound deck from which we built epic, wooden train tracks, witnessed double rainbows, monsoon lightning strikes, and observed gila monsters, snakes, deer, javelina families, coyotes, bobcats, quail, and rabbits. We said goodbye to Mount Lemmon, the hiking trails, our "beach," saguaros, prickly pears, the mesquite, and palo verde. We hooted a goodbye to the owls that echoed our final evening adieu. We said goodbye to the restaurants that knew us by name, the friends we grew up with, our cycling and running buddies, and the grandparents and other family members who visited with us every week. We said goodbye to the close group of people who loved us but could not erase what was on the Internet. Amy looked back on our empty home on Soldier Trail (ST) and wrote these words:

> *That home inside those walls holds our story—a love story so beautifully scripted that I think the walls were gifted our presence. I hope those walls will learn a new love story and that the next family will find ST to be a home worthy of housing their memories. It's hard to let go. In fact, I would say it's a visceral pain. But today I cried because the memories were so perfectly beautiful. I cried because time is slipping and our boys are growing up*

way too fast. And I cried because I now recognize that ST is nothing more than where our stories were written.

It will likely be one of the best chapters we will ever write because in that home we became six. We wrote the chapters that helped us become who we are now. But the story is still being written. Just housed in new walls. ST is now part of that memory. An empty house. Not a home. Seeing it empty made me feel what my life would be like without you guys. Completely void and empty. Wherever you guys are is where my home is and where I want the next chapters of my story written.

Tucson no longer felt like home. It no longer felt safe and accepting. It had carried us until it was time to leave the nest, and that time was now. We climbed into the RV (aptly named Shadow Cruiser in memory of our dog) with adventurous spirits enveloping sadness and disgrace. Our new adventure would take us to places few have been, to places we never would have traversed without the catalyst of my YouTube protest. That moment would prove to be an event we sometimes would call a curse and sometimes a blessing, but an event we would not have chosen of our own accord. This was happening whether we liked it or not. Our ability to see it for what it was would be a long, hard lesson to learn.

We lost a life we had worked over fifteen years to build. We had lost more than money. We had lost our control; we had lost the safety we thought we had.

We had built a dream on a foundation with a false sense of security evidenced by the fact that it all came crashing down in two-and-one-half minutes.

Chapter 12
Thanksgiving

Due to my harried and hurried departure from Vante, I never got to say goodbye to my Vante family. I was sorry for how they had been impacted and wished I had been able to properly say goodbye to them in person. I wrote my goodbye letter a couple weeks after being fired, but out of fear I did not send it to them. This is the letter I regretfully held on to and hope finds its way to them through this book:

> *One of the hardest parts of this ordeal was the loss of what I consider to be my work family at Vante. The reaction to my choices has caused you a lot of grief and embarrassment. You don't deserve the consequences of my actions. Only I do. If any customers or vendors are reading this right now and are considering ending your business relationship with Vante, please don't. They don't deserve it. They are beautiful people. They work very hard for you. They want to make your experience full of value. Please keep giving them your business.*
>
> *Vante, because I do consider you my family, I want to say goodbye formally to you. In the interest of keeping the following people out of harm's way, instead of providing your specific name, I'll try to use unique words that will clue you in as to who I am addressing.*

Starting with my staff. You are the best team any CFO could ever have. So thorough, responsive, and friendly. I could always depend on you. We had such a small team, yet we were able to accomplish so much, and not only quickly but accurately. My replacement will definitely realize how lucky they are to have such a solid group supporting them. To the only gentleman on my team, thank you for being so dependable. You are an accounting machine. I hope you stumble upon a priceless gem. To my collections DSO warrior, you nearly single-handedly changed our cash position over the last 2 ½ years. You should be so proud. To my LLC and ESOP guru, as I have said in the past, I couldn't ask for a more well-rounded individual. I could ask you for anything and, even if you had no prior experience in the random financial and accounting requests I made of you, you always pulled it off with an unmatched logic and level of thoroughness. I also think you are a wonderful mother.

To the shipping, inventory and inspection folks, thank you for being so patient on my first and last try to paint those hundreds of metal plates. I know you had to redo most of them, but you never made me feel bad about it. Thank you.

To repair and assemblers, I'll miss your constant upbeat smiles, for sure.

To the machine shop, you guys are ridiculous. The level of quality that comes out of your shop is amazing. Customers recognize it and so does everyone at Vante.

To the fantasy football crew, I so would have taken your money this year. Thanks for teaching me how to play fantasy football in the first place. If you still let me in your pool, watch out! I have so much free time on my hands right now that I might actually stand a chance of winning.

To the Ambassador of Shenanigans, I'll be hoping for the Penguins to make it to the Stanly Cup next year.

To my political opposite, our time at the gala is a great memory. I'm going to miss our many debates.

To my wellness room comrade, please complete the building improvements we were working on. They will make everyone feel better about where they work, particularly now. Oh, and don't give up on the solar idea. It would reflect on the company's progressiveness and social awareness.

To all the engineers, thank you so much for taking the time to teach me the technical side of the business. Two things I learned while working with you: One, you people are wicked smart and, two, I am not cut out to be an engineer. Just couldn't keep up with you.

To Quality, thank you for always being so positive and friendly. I'll work on my foosball just for you.

To the Ambassador of Awesomeness. You and your team have worked your butts off to get our output to where it is today. I remember our lunch at El Charro last year. You said you left work sometimes not knowing if it was good enough. But you said that if it wasn't, at least you knew you did your best. Dude, your best was so good enough. And the people that you manage couldn't have a more genuine person looking out for them.

To the Director of First Impressions, the best start to every morning at Vante for me was your "good morning." I'm so sorry you had to hear all of those voicemails.

To the funniest HR rep on the planet, I am going to miss your emails. Your emails were distinct, for when you sent them, moments later the entire building would erupt in unified laughter. You are exactly what Vante needs right now.

To HR, I still remember the first question you asked me in my interview 2 ½ years ago. You asked me what was the most important thing to me at a company. I took less than a second to say that it was "the people." I really meant that. I know I meant that because the hardest part to swallow in this whole ordeal is how Vante's employees have been affected. Thank you for the confidence and friendship. You are Vante's MVP.

To "manufacturing," I sure could have used the calmness and poise you always seem to exude under even the most stressful circumstances. It's so clear you love your kids unconditionally. It was a pleasure working side-by-side with you.

To my Brother Bean, you are a beautiful human being. Thank you for the call of encouragement. I really do love you like a brother.

To my former boss, getting to know you on a personal level was not something you let just anyone do. I learned about leadership, strategy, and even finance from you. You are a pillar in the Tucson community and, for my part, I am so

> *sorry that I put you in this position. You taught me so much and gave me so much confidence.*
>
> *To all of you, if you stay focused on the last two months of the fiscal year, you'll have pulled off the strongest financial year in the company's history in the midst of possibly the most disruptive. So much to be proud of.*
>
> *Good luck and I will miss you,*
> *Adam*
> *Your Ambassador of Kwan (Love, Respect, Community, and the Dollars too)*

I can't tell you the relief I feel in finally sharing this.

It took a solid week to properly say goodbye to our Tucson life. Meeting after meeting, we visited with our friends and family to embrace, reminisce, and grieve. Depending on their beliefs, everyone had different opinions on the protest and ensuing backlash, but everyone agreed we would bounce back quickly. We were a family of survivors. We shared their certainty.

At the end of August 2012, in a packed RV my family and I traveled north to spend time in nature beginning with the Grand Canyon and ending in Edwardsville, Illinois, where we stayed with my in-laws to reset and recharge.

We home schooled the boys during the two months we wandered, visiting cities we had always thought we would like to move to if we didn't have all of our fortune captive in Vante. Now we were able to choose to move anywhere we had desired. Amy had been fantasizing about a move to Portland for years now, and the Pacific Northwest somehow felt right. Upon a sight-seeing visit to Portland, we were enamored with the kindness of the people. Cars stopped abruptly if any person was even near a crosswalk. When we asked for directions, strangers would walk the blocks to literally show us the way. Even grocery shopping was enjoyable at the New Seasons grocery store down the road where they truly were, "The Friendliest Grocery Store in Town." People recycled, composted, raised chickens, posted poetry and free little libraries in their front yards, looked you in the eyes, smiled for no apparent reason, and advocated boldly for human rights. "Portland is where young people come to retire," I was told by the recruiter I met there.

I was drawn to the energy of this quirky city and decided to interview for a job. Halloween was a few days away and the interview went so well that I stayed for the second and third round interviews while the family traveled back to Edwardsville to prepare for the move.

Before interviewing I was counseled by an attorney and colleagues as to how to handle the “chicken incident.” Unanimously, I was advised to focus on the fifteen years of my career and not to mention the video. “Your employer should focus on your career and not your personal stand for human rights.” This was the counsel I accepted, the counsel which suited my eagerness to move past the embarrassing and irrational events in August. I would let my business skills decide my fate, not my social media mishap.

A letter of recommendation from my former CEO was vital in winning this competitive position, as some of the internet comments begged the question as to why I would get fired for such a relatively mild and personal protest. Some speculated that Vante must have had other reasons to get rid of me and used the chicken incident as the opportunity to do so. Imagining how all of this might have impacted him, I expected my former CEO would be reluctant, so I called him up and literally begged him to focus on my time *before* the incident, before my “error in judgment,” as he described it. I begged loudly and honestly, reminding him of the praise he bestowed upon me during so many meetings and how he and Vante’s board had approved my largest tranche of restricted stock just two weeks before he fired me. I told him how my boys needed the medical benefits and how hard it would be to win a leadership role without the praise of my previous boss. I experienced how the word "grovel" deficiently describes actually doing so. One grovels when one has no other choice, when one feels helpless and needs a drop of grace. I asked him what I could do for that letter. I told him I would do anything and my desperation proved it. I wasn't going to give up by hanging up. He would have to hang up on me. I knew he could find the memory of my performance. It was there. He just needed to look past the video. After a long, uncomfortable pause, he said he would be willing to write a letter of recommendation.

A few days later, after vetting it through his attorney, he emailed me the recommendation letter.

And with that, I landed the job!

I received an offer from an IPO-bound company that managed real estate, a salary that matched my Vante earnings, and potential equity, so we once again packed and drove our RV across the country to Portland, Oregon—to the city of roses and bridges, phenomenal food, award-winning microbrews and coffee, and kind people. We had income, medical benefits, and a new beginning.

During my first two weeks at the new job things were moving fast. I was included in executive meetings, given much responsibility and I had begun to assemble and hire a team to run the company's pricing department. Five years in IBM's pricing and investment analysis department had given me ample experience from which to draw. I was rebuilding, but I knew I was back—back to making six figures, back to saving, spending, and giving. I was also in a toxic working environment. Water cooler talk consisted of the retelling of an incident that had happened a few months prior to my hiring. One of the top executives had berated two employees for not following his instructions that would have clearly violated an HR policy.

I asked if anyone had tried to diffuse the situation. No one wanted to lose their jobs so everyone just remained silently hidden in their cubicles during the rampage. Later, over twenty employees chose to report him to HR claiming a hostile work environment. He was forced by the company's chief counsel to write an apology. The female worker was moved to another floor of their building. A week later the executive was promoted to president.

I wondered how long I would last at a place like this. I asked myself what I would have done if I had been an employee at this time and had personally witnessed the lashing. I had paid a hefty price for imperfectly standing up for human rights just few months ago. I considered myself lucky not to have observed such abuse in the midst of trying to rebuild my own livelihood and safety. Given my circumstances, I felt voiceless. I needed this job.

Thanksgiving 2012 was truly a time full of things for which to be grateful. We had moved twice and were getting our first paycheck in over three months, and now we were preparing to move into our new affluent neighborhood where we hoped to remain for a few years. We were making new friends and exploring our new city. The boys' medical needs soon would be covered by my new employer, whose initial feedback after my first week to the recruiter that helped me get the job was, "Adam is doing great. Feels like he's going to be an excellent hire." We had survived the three month storm together. We felt stronger—wounded but stronger. We missed our Tucson family and missed our familiar life but were thankful we could care for ourselves.

The Monday following Thanksgiving was quiet in the office. Many people had taken the day off to enjoy time with out-of-town guests, but I felt pressure to deliver quick results from my new, developing team. It was six o'clock in the evening and I was heading out the door to catch dinner with the family when my boss, the CFO, called me into his office. The company's legal counsel—the same person who forced the new president to apologize—was already sitting at the small, round table that the CFO and I joined. The CFO explained that before the Thanksgiving break someone had Googled my name. Doing an Internet search for "Adam Smith" had always generated pages and pages of the 18th century "Father of Economics" also born on June 5th, but 254 years earlier. Ever since Chick-fil-A Appreciation Day, my information topped the Father of Economics. I was easy to find and my story was unpleasant. The CFO told me my video had gone viral within the company and that I had lied to them during the interview process. I replied that I wasn't legally obligated to disclose information about the video. His eyes darted to his legal counsel, who nodded in agreement. Nevertheless, the CFO had already made arrangements prior to questioning me. He told me that I should pack up my things and leave.

I drove home slowly during this commute. About halfway home, I pulled over and parked in an empty lot, placed my head on the same steering wheel I had gripped while recording my protest, listened to my deep sighs, and felt my body painfully caving in on itself with my chest at the core of the tightening. I didn't have the courage to call Amy with the news that I had been fired from three jobs in less than four months. I was not ready to admit that the consequences of my protest were larger than I could have imagined. I did not want to pay any more for this mistake, so before bringing home the news I called a recruiter working for a national firm for help and scheduled a meeting for the following week. At least I could offer Amy a glimmer of hope to help balance this latest blow.

We couldn't believe it. We had moved to Portland, the kids' were in a new school trying to make new friends, and we felt we had paid enough for the protest. I tried to balance the bad news with the good news of the recruiter meeting, but it was short-lived. The day before the meeting, I received a call from the recruiter. She also happened to be contracted with the company from which I had just been fired. They had called her the day before for help locating a new executive to replace a liar named Adam Smith. The recruiter reprimanded me, told me to never call her company or office again and canceled my meeting. Portland felt like a small town where everybody knows your name. The taste of the beginning moments of depression was bitter. I felt bruised. Given the holiday slowdown, I realized getting a new job would not happen until 2013.

Chapter 13
The Scarlet Name

In early 2013 I secured an interview and subsequent offer for the CFO role of a family-owned wireless company in Portland. Having learned from my November firing that non-disclosure of my Chick-fil-A video was detrimental, I intentionally met with the CEO to disclose the public firings and now the Thanksgiving firing. I showed him the recommendation letter from my former CEO. The CEO and I spoke all day and he jovially laughed at the craziness I had experienced. He considered himself an open-minded conservative who hated Obama, loved his guns, and had a gay family member he had witnessed being harassed for his sexual orientation. My new CEO and I shook hands. He stated that he had no need to see the Chick-fil-A video and reiterated that he appreciated my honesty and the CFO offer remained. He introduced me to the rest of the executive team, including the VP of Sales who happened to live one block up from me. We made arrangements to carpool on my first day.

That night, on my way home from successfully sharing my scandalous public firing and feeling accepted in spite of what was on the Internet, I stopped at the grocery store to purchase a bottle of celebratory wine. I would deliver the big news to Amy in person and with gusto. We put the boys to bed, telling them the great news then finished the bottle of wine on the couch in front of the fire and held each other in relief and contentment. Everything was right with the world. We slept so soundly that night. Maybe it was the expensive wine, maybe it was the release of coming out of hiding, maybe it was the ensuing paycheck headed our way. Regardless of what it was, there was rest for the weary.

The next morning, I began to tie up any personal loose ends before my first week back in the working world, including informing my recruiters that I had accepted an offer and would no longer be needing their services. After thanking my recruiters for their support, I opened my inbox and found an email from the new junior HR representative of the wireless company. I thought that perhaps the email was a new employee orientation package. I was anxious to sign up for benefits and direct deposits so I opened the email with a light exuberance. But the email was not welcoming. It was dismissing, literally, "We regret to inform you that after careful consideration, we will continue our search for a new CFO. We wish you both personal and professional success in your job search and in the future."

Stunned and in disbelief I called the wireless CEO to talk. His receptionist said he was unavailable all day and the day after that. I sent an email to him asking to meet to discuss his concerns. He never replied or called back.

After many more months of searching, I had amassed a strong network of headhunters and many first round interviews, but when the protest was mentioned, the interview process would cease. One after another. I was not used to being rejected for jobs, not with the kind of resume and credentials I had accumulated. It was very humbling.

Initially I focused on permanent, full-time roles. That was proving to be unsuccessful, so my recruiters suggested I open up my search to temporary roles, as there would be no need to disclose the protest fiasco, giving me time to impress my temporary bosses into, hopefully, a full-time permanent role.

The strategy worked. I quickly received temporary work at a national bike rental company whose Controller and CFO had recently put in their notices. They were to train me during their final week. On the fourth day of training, the outgoing CFO called me into his office and told me that I wasn't learning fast enough and that he questioned whether I could even close the books later that month. His initial assessment seemed charged and baseless. I calmly asked what it would take to prove to him that this recent CPA and former CFO could absolutely, without a doubt, close the monthly books. I was confident I could perform this simple task as I had done thirty times in the thirty months I was employed at Vante. There was no test offered to me. I was dismissed.

By now I had become a professional stuffer of job rejections. I had been rejected or let go so many times within the last six months, I was able to stuff the emotion down if it meant presenting myself as stable during an interview. However, the emotional baggage was piling up and I had become exhausted at stuffing more and more into the dark. Our retirement savings were dwindling. My spirit was diminishing. But I had a role to play. I was the provider. The show must go on.

And it did. Interview after interview ended with the same "We'll get back to you" response. They never got back to me and I was never given reasons. It was Groundhog Day over and over and over again. I could land the interview, make great connections during the interviews, but when Chick-fil-A was mentioned, the interviewer's energy would change. Sometimes they became colder and the interview would end abruptly. Other times, the interviewer would become warmer, and some even remembered seeing me on television. Some interviewers went as far as to thank me for my sacrifice. I was never witness to the moment that enthusiasm waned for them. But it always did. Every. Single. Time. I had nearly a dozen interviews, all resulting in silence. No explanations.

In the summer of 2013, I landed a temp role that lasted for ten weeks at a technology company. After the first three weeks, employees were asking me whether I would be interested in a full-time role. I was sure they had not yet Googled me. I remember having to close myself in the employee bathroom when a rush of anxiety would overtake me during the workday. I was afraid that at any moment, someone in the organization might become bored and curious as to who the new guy was. I was always one Internet search away from another pink slip.

I was interested in any role at this point. It had been many months since there had been steady work and the job hunting, interviewing, and rejections, were all so exhausting. As much as I wanted a role, I knew I would have to be honest about my past year of firings and I was pretty confident that would not fly with this company run by Mormons. I did secretly hope that they would value my business skills and maybe even sympathize with a man punished heavily for publicly voicing his beliefs. I hoped they would find grace to show this man who protested poorly. The permanent job talks died down near the eighth week. I was beginning to feel I was the only person not privy to the full truth.

Luckily, during that time I had continued my search for a full-time role and nabbed an interview for a controller position at a pool equipment manufacturer. My resume was submitted late in their hiring process, but because my credentials were so stellar, the hiring CFO decided it was worth the disruption to the other two candidates that were weeks ahead of me in the interview process. I interviewed on a Thursday with the CFO. He asked direct questions and I disclosed everything. I even made him watch the YouTube video with me and we viewed some of the more sensationalized stories together. I felt he could see right through the media circus, and straight into the heart of the true me. He was smart too. He recognized the caliber of the training from which my career had been built and told me that his main concern was how long I would stay with the company. He correctly theorized that after being with his company for six months, my situation would look less risky to other companies. He sensed I would use his company as a temporary landing space while I searched for more money elsewhere. He also knew he was offering half the salary and no equity to which I had been accustomed. Knowing I had to make a sacrifice, I promised him, in complete genuineness, that I would stay with his company for a minimum of two years, simply out of gratitude for giving me a chance when no one else was willing. I had every intention of keeping this promise. We shook hands and I left wondering if I would get the second and final interviews.

The next day I met all the executives, including one who started the interview with, "I can't believe *you* are here, looking for a job with this company! I told my wife last night about you and we both can't wait to have you and your family over for dinner! You are a hero, Adam. You are a hero." The other executives had similar interviews with me, except the CEO, who seemed in a rush to leave for a noon tee time. He asked me if I was going to be talking about gay rights at the workplace. I told him my views are my own and I had no interest in creating any drama. He seemed satisfied and left the decision to hire to the CFO.

At noon on Friday, the hiring CFO literally had a candidate in the office next to him waiting for an offer. I had crept into the process so late that the CFO had a decision to make at that moment. He and I went into his office to discuss his dilemma. First, I acknowledged the anxiety he must be feeling around this decision. I wasn't trying to control him. I knew that if he was going to take this stand to hire me and not rescind an offer, then he would need to do so on his own terms without pressure from me. He explained the internal conflict he was feeling. He felt the other candidate was the safer choice and that hiring me may actually put his job in jeopardy, as he felt I was more qualified than he to be CFO. He recalled the MBA lesson he learned to hire people more talented than him, to build a team of the highest caliber without fear. I asked him a most important question, "What does your gut say?" Immediately he answered, "You."

We agreed on a salary and the minimum two year commitment, shook hands, and he told me I would receive the formal letter that evening. He was certain of his decision and his certainty fed mine. I was going to enjoy working for such a genuine, hard-working man.

I did not stop on the way home this time. I did not even wait to reach home before sharing the desperately good news with Amy. I called her and could barely speak. I had been so low during this past year, so desperate, so broken. Amy was at first skeptical and guarded. We had experienced great disappointment at moments like these. We were both tired of being slung around like a toy yo-yo. I described the CFO's certainty, the firmness in his handshake, the long eye contact and the genuine, kind spirit of this man. I told her that I was grateful to him and meant to keep my two-year promise regardless of any subsequent offers that may follow. I was experiencing so much elation while talking to her that I hadn't even noticed the call I missed. I had reached the front door and was wrapped in the congratulatory arms of my family. The missed call was from an unknown caller. And there was a new voicemail:

Hey Adam, I just wanted to call and let you know that I've had a couple people express some concerns and I've done a little more looking on the Internet . . . I think you are going to be successful in whatever you do, but I need to figure out if this is going to personally cost me or be a distraction."

Two days later, the CFO called to say my offer had been rescinded.

*****

How was Adam Smith going to get a job? How was Adam Smith even going to land an interview when the simplest Google search portrayed him as an attacking, harassing bully deserving of public humiliation?

I became gridlocked in fear and anxiety. I was afraid to mention my last name to neighbors, afraid to answer the common question, "So what brought you to Portland?," afraid to fill out the background check to coach my boys' little league team, afraid to apply for jobs, afraid to share too intimately with new acquaintances, afraid that people would judge me before giving me a chance, afraid to just be human.

I remember one incident when a young man was driving very fast and recklessly in a parking lot and nearly hit one of my sons. I yelled at him to slow down and my chest immediately tightened. My eyes darted around in panic and I quickly silenced myself even though he was putting people in danger. I was afraid of any confrontation, even justified confrontations. I was afraid that at any moment someone would video tape me and send another message across the media to perpetuate the story that Adam Smith was indeed the vile villain everyone believed him to be. I became afraid of living, of always being watched, afraid of making any mistake. I was not allowed to make a mistake. I had heard society's message abundantly clear: there was no room for mistakes.

I wished people would judge me on my career and for the kind of person I was outside those 2.5 minutes. When the media would call, Amy would be so frustrated with them, wishing they would look at the real story. She wished she could tell them that if they wanted to know the truth they'd look at the bigger picture. They'd see our contributions to our community, our love for children, our commitment to giving back. They wouldn't paint a monster out of a loving man. She saw me when I could no longer see myself. I needed more people like her. I needed people to judge me on more than sensationalized headlines and the vicious opinions of strangers. I was willing to change anything to provide for my family, even my name.

In an attempt to get people to see me and not the internet-me, I began using my middle name on my resume and in every new introduction instead. Mark, a name my father tried to use to redeem himself, a name I would now use to try to do the same. I slowly began to inform those who knew me as Adam that I would now be called Mark. Amy changed my name on all of her previous blog posts and practiced getting comfortable with my new name. The boys were confused as to why their dad was now suddenly calling himself by a name they did not recognize. My youngest told his new school that his daddy's name was now Mark and they were not to call him Adam. That prompted the school to call and question me as it sent up many understandable red flags. I was definitely hiding and red flags were firing inside of me too. We were actively making an effort to change my identity with something as simple as erasing the name Adam from our personal life. Becoming Mark seemed like a small price to pay in order to create a little space between us and Adam's mistake.

This may seem relatively easy. One may ask what the big deal was. Many people change their names. But it was more than that. Using the name Mark was strange. I felt like I was hiding. I was hiding. I felt as though I was lying every time the name left my lips. The beginning of each new relationship started with a Mark mask.

The death of the Adam Smith name felt like a literal death. I had liked my name. My name was dear to me. All my achievements were in Adam's name, not Mark's.

I fell into an abyss of darkness, an abyss without even a sliver of light this time. I was alone. Nobody knew who I was. Not even me. Subconsciously, I had made the decision never to be seen again. With a rationalization that I needed to feed my family at all costs, I donned the darkest, heaviest mask of my life, and that mask would quickly suffocate me.

One morning I had to do something to feed my family that felt like stealing. Groceries were needed and there wasn't any more money left in the retirement accounts. Their balances all read "$0.01." One penny left to avoid the $25 fee to close the account. I asked the Fidelity rep how long the account could stay at $0.01. He said, "Forever."

When the checking, savings, and retirement accounts hit a penny something happened inside me. I went for a walk in the new neighborhood we had recently moved to, a cheaper rental house fifty yards from rumbling train tracks that constantly reminded me of the downward trajectory of our struggles. In the middle of the walk, away from the thunderous engines, I felt a wave crash inside of me. Urges to take from those who had more than me surfaced, from those people who seem so carefree and safe. I felt this craving so strong and deep, it was instinctual—how I imagine a wolf feels when it is time to hunt to keep from watching its cubs whine, suffer, wither, and decay.

The image of what was to come if circumstances did not soon change was vivid, full of detail. I imagined myself in a grocery store, looking both ways and then grabbing of a loaf of bread and slipping it inside my coat. Then I imagined trying to assuage the wave for more than a meal time by taking the BMW I'd just walked past to the shady mechanic down the street, and hoping my instincts were correct that the place was a chop shop ready to hand me a few thousand dollars for a fifteen-minute job.

I wanted the kill to be quick because I was feeling everything I was imagining. My entire body felt heavy, sick, distorted, and pitiful. I ached to the bones and my stomach churned with the death of love, the smothering of love, of me, my essence. I felt myself turning into a wild, desperate animal.

I thought, *Best to stay legal, for now. There's one last place I can go without risking a run in with authorities—a place where I can close the door and click on a mouse. It will only take fifteen minutes.*

I walked back home, opened the office door, and went to the Fidelity website that showed my $0.01 IRA accounts. I scrolled down and saw more digits. Four lines, each with about five thousand dollars next to their names—my sons' education accounts, money set aside specifically for them, their futures, not for their food and shelter.

And then a painful question crept in: *From whose account should I withdraw?* The oldest, the twins, or the youngest? The youngest made most sense, as it would give me more time to replenish, but would he eventually find out that I chose him first to take from? And would he imagine I chose him because I loved him less? Would he be capable of seeing the rationale—the rationale to take from your children, exchanging their future for their present?

What kind of father lets this happen? What kind of father fucks up so badly that he must take from his children? I didn't hear or see anyone on Facebook posting this type of entry, probably out of fear of being unfollowed, unliked. I mean who wants that kind of energy? Or maybe I was the only one. Who wants to hear about suffering when we all are trying to avoid it so desperately?

I made my thieving mouse clicks and then a message pops up, "You must call to withdraw from this 529 savings account." My breathing stopped. I was capable of making a secret mouse click, but to verbalize what I intended to do to a stranger was too much vulnerability and shame for me at that moment.

I left the computer and found Amy. I needed her wings to hold me in a place of non-judgment, of acceptance, of love. I needed to hear that things were going to be okay between us, that she loved me in spite of my taking from our children.

As I was held in those wings, I was able to forget about all the things that were not supposed to be happening. I was able to feel temporary relief from a repeating story being played in my mind. The story that I was a thief, a beggar, a liar, less than, a failure, a mistake.

SECTION THREE

KNOW THYSELF

No man for any considerable period
can wear one face to himself and another to the
multitude, without finally getting bewildered as to which
may be the true.

—Nathaniel Hawthorne, *The*
Scarlet Letter, 1850

Chapter 14
I'm A Mistake

One thing I know I'm good at is math. A multitude of first- and second-round interviews with companies and recruiters followed with silent rejections, plus three firings, two rescinded offers, and two early dismissals, equals darkness. As someone who has waded into dark, brown metal boxes behind grocery stores to find food, I know how to survive. It takes a lot to push a survivor to the point of giving up.

Yet, here I was, unemployed with a prestigious resume and a willingness to work for just about anyone who would have me and, for the first time since I started working the corner on my own at ten years old, I could not provide for my family. Flashbacks to my dumpster diving days actually gifted me a strange calmness. I knew that if it came to it, I would slide that brown door open again and forage like a hungry child. No one would starve as long as I was alive. However, lonely months of job searching followed by cold rejections added something to the equation for which I could not account. The heavy toll of depression.

Depressive math, a subject if offered in college would have no takers, consumed me as the one-year anniversary of the Chick-fil-A protest grew closer. My mind arbitrarily, as minds like to do, chose the one-year anniversary to replay and repeat dark mantras. I doubted that even a Buddhist master could silence the voice inside my mind. It said in a cold, bold, devilish tone, "I made a mistake." It repeated that mantra over and over again until it eventually morphed into, "I am a mistake." My mind pushed me down this mistaken, misshapen, dark hole and it began to contemplate a mathematical solution that seemed logical to a desperate man reliving a depth of rejection once experienced as a boy who witnessed his father signing away parental rights—a father boldly and willingly releasing his not-so-redeeming, disappointment of a son: Adam Mark.

My mind's solution was to follow the values of any reasonable corporation, maximize profit by triggering an event that would pay my family the one million dollars we lost and was still available from my term life insurance policy. I considered making the exchange of my pitiful, mistake-filled life for my wife and sons' financial comfort, and to ease the journey on which I found myself. An "accidental" missed turn on a high mountain pass near the Oregon Coast is all it would take. No one could know my intention or else the policy would be nullified by the suicide clause, leaving the family with nothing. No, this mathematical solution would need to be completed in shadow with no witnesses, no one but me in that dark metal bin, no one but me to make my last "mistake." My previous experience in metal boxes made me the perfect fit for this job—an offer that couldn't be rescinded, and one I honestly contemplated in the darkest parts of my mind.

In August 2013, on the one year mark of my fall, I rode my bike up the 2.5 mile steep, wooded, paved road to Washington Park, around the circular trail of the Vietnam Memorial. My fingers traced the names of the deceased veterans etched deep inside the granite slabs. I was overcome with grief, regret, shame, pain. I set my bike in the grass and lay beside it. Something inside me told me to record what I was going to say out loud. I pulled out the same iPhone I used to tape my protest one year ago and I video recorded a belief that had haunted me since childhood, "I am a mistake."

Emotionally drained, that night I drank myself to sleep as my mind incessantly replayed its most logical answer to this mess, I was worth more dead than alive. But, there was one element to the logical equation that my mind's million dollar solution did not consider. I married a light that shone brightest in darkest times. I was married to an angel who watched my most recent, one year struggle into darkness, and, as she had for so many years previously, took action from her heart.

I woke up the next morning with a splitting headache to find dozens of letters laminated and bound together. Amy had helplessly witnessed my downward spiral, and even though I chose not to share my mind's math with her, she knew I was drowning and needed saving. She had reached out to friends and family a few weeks prior to the one year anniversary asking them to write personal letters of encouragement. She was hoping that letters of love would shine enough light to reach me in my shadows.

There I lay, a mess of a man. Hopeless. My angel combing her fingers through my unkempt hair, whispering words of encouragement just as my mom used to do. She was doing everything she could to ease my burdens. I knew she wanted me to read those letters right then, to fill myself with the soothing, loving words, to feel embraced. But I was too far gone. There was nothing but darkness.

A few days passed before I reached for those letters. I asked Amy to read them to me because when I tried, I could only read the first few words before I was blinded by their light and my tears.

She recited the words of unconditional, pure love from familiar but forgotten voices:

- *"What defines you is not your job or title or any of that BS. It's what's inside you."*

- *"It's impossible to be in the same room with you and not feel energized by your personality, and nothing will ever change that."*

- *"I admire you and your family and I always will."*

- *"Don't allow one event in a life full of events define who you are. And allow yourself to celebrate who you are."*

- *"The real failure is to be silent. I think you are an amazing man/husband/father . . ."*

- *"I share the disbelief, anger and sadness with others who cannot fathom why anyone wouldn't see past the few minutes of that unfortunate video to the decent, caring, intelligent person you are."*

- *"The first word that comes to mind when your name is mentioned is passion. The second word that comes to mind is compassion."*

- *"You are passionate, compassionate, warm, friendly, determined, committed, and courageous."*

- *"These recent changes in your lives doesn't matter to us. The Adam we first met and have grown to like is an amazing man and father."*

- *"You have shown and proven over the years that you have the qualities that make men great. You show love and care to those less fortunate and are always an encouragement to others."*

- *"You wear your heart on your sleeve which is an enduring characteristic of someone who is not ashamed of who he is."*

- *"You have a real strength of character and passion for pursuing what you believe in. May you always pursue life with zeal and never give up."*

- *"Please know that you are not defined by one action but the many wonderful things you have done and continue to do."*

- *"I was working for such a wonderful family that was so giving and all they cared about was giving to others. This made me so happy and thankful. Thank you for being you."*

- *"Your generosity and support have always kept a bright light shining in my life."*

- *"I encourage you to reach within yourself, go back to that young man starting out, determined to make a good life for himself and his family. It's in you."*

- *"One thing has remained constant, and now shines brighter than ever before; you are a man of conviction. A passion for the right thing. A passion to be good, true and strong."*

- *"My wish for you on this one year anniversary is that you find peace and acceptance with what your life has now become. Because it still kicks ass! You guys still rock!"*

Those kind, warm words were in stark contrast to the words I had spent the last year reading on the Internet, listening to in rescinded offers and replies of silence, and hearing from the manipulative, mathematical voice in my head. Amy's angelic tone reading such words of love and encouragement pierced through all logic and the light began to reach my heart that was crying out, "There is truth beyond these letters, these rejections, these stories."

That day I searched for help and, as synchronicity would have it, a six-day Intensive Journal workshop was being offered in Seattle two weeks from then, the same workshop that carried me through my exodus from my fundamental religious beliefs five years earlier. I found a reason to wait a few more weeks before executing my million-dollar plan.

Chapter 15
Devil Preacher

I confided in my two therapists about my mathematical option and how hopeless I felt. They independently assessed that I should attend the workshop. One of my therapists, who was very familiar with C.G. Jung and Ira Progoff's[13] psychotherapeutic work, suggested I create an image I could take with me to the workshop—an image of my negative self-talk that kept repeating, "I am a mistake. I am a mistake."

Instantly, I knew what it looked like, a devil-looking figure, abstract pointed nose, long snake tongue, surrounded by fire and standing behind the familiar pulpit that stood above the small pool of water where an almost seven-year-old boy was submerged, and baptized thirty years ago to circumvent the age of accountability, and douse the threat of eternal fire.

I resisted drawing the image until the day before I left for the workshop. Using my sons' colored pencils, I sat at the warped white wooden table recently purchased from Goodwill for ten dollars, and I began to draw.

I drew and drew, wishing the kids hadn't lost so many of the pencils, for I kept reaching for distinct, specific colors. I looked, I drew, I stopped. Repeat. Repeat. The picture just flowed out of me, easily, effortlessly. It didn't look like a Rembrandt, but it was authentic, detailed, and relevant to me. I knew this image intimately.

I was going to "dialogue" with this entity at the workshop, and having an image would make the "meeting" a face-to-face encounter, the kind of meeting where a real connection could happen.

Progoff *Intensive Journal* Workshop for Self-Development

At an *Intensive Journal* workshop, one begins writing unfiltered and without judgment, about what is real at this moment in life. Even if what is written does not sound nice, strong or perfect it is written. You write as though no one else would read it. Without editing, without thinking or rationalization you write anything that is naturally coming up.

The following are not the full exercises of the workshop, but commentary and select excerpts of what poured out of me over the course of the six days. In the spirit of the workshop and for purposes of the reader to experience what this workshop authentically looked like, most of my writing has been left unedited.

Day One

"A special value of the *Intensive Journal* approach is that it enables individuals to break through situations of stalemate where their lives had seemed to have reached a dead end."[14]

Personal Commentary: I came to the workshop on August 18, 2013 with a drawing of a Devil Preacher. I knew self-doubt/negative self-talk (Devil Preacher) would show itself during this time of soul searching. I felt stuck in ALL areas of my life. The workshop's facilitators, Evelyn and Carol, began the workshop with the question, "Where am I in the movement of my life?"

My Life Now *August 18, 2013*

I am unemployed. Have been so for 12 months and 16 days.

This is a time when I am the father of four sons and married to Amy for over 16 years.

This is a time in my life where I am 36 years old.

This is a time when I am at a crossroads, not only in my career but also in my life.

This is a time in my life where I moved to Portland, Oregon from Tucson, Arizona about a year ago.

This is a time in my life where I am questioning everything: my past, present, and future.

This is a time in my life where I find myself crying frequently at the smallest of things.
This is a time in my life where I feel a tightening in my chest almost constantly.
This is a time in my life where I have no job and running out of money.
This is a time in my life where a sense of freedom and imprisonment meet.
This is a time in my life where an August 1, 2012 YouTube video keeps me from being hired, where I have received multiple offers and then have had them taken away.
This is a time in my life where I have lost 20 pounds over the last year, lighter than when I was in high school.
This is a time in my life where my mind tells me that I am worth more dead than alive.
This is a time in my life where I sense my heart has some things to say but is muted by noisy, incessant thoughts of poor me, of poor, wretched, worthless little me.

Day Two

Commentary: "Dialoguing" in the workshop is a process by which you write as though you are transcribing a dialogue between two people. Typically, the dialogue is between you and another person, an event, your work, society or your own body. I chose to dialogue with my wife, Amy. She and I had been in marriage therapy for the past year, trying to weather the storm in which we found ourselves.

<u>*Dialogue with Amy* *August 19, 2013*</u>

Amy: I really hope you get better soon. I am struggling with holding our family and myself together. I need you.
Me: Yes, I see that you need me. I need you too.
Amy: I have been through a lot, Adam. I just don't know how much more I can take.
Me: Yes, I see.
Amy: How are we going to make it through this?
Me: How do you think we will?
Amy: I don't know. I feel like I've lost hope for us, for you, but I keep staying because we have kids that need us to stick together and make this work.

"Once you have learned how to use it, the *Intensive Journal* method becomes like a musical instrument you can play; and its melodies are the themes and the intimations of meaning in your life. Going to great heights and to great depths, the life music that persons find themselves playing upon their *Intensive Journal* Instruments is often startling. They did not expect to find in themselves sounds of such strength or such sweetness, such sensitivity in the midst of pain, such capacities for harmony or such inner vision."

Next, I dialogued with my oldest son, Sterling.

Dialogue with Sterling *August 19, 2013*

Me: Hello Sterling. I'm sure you are not surprised to know that I chose you to dialogue with. I have seen deep wisdom come from within you. I recall your clarity when I asked you about whether we should adopt Gibson. And, so now I come to you again for wisdom.

Sterling: Hi, Dad. You don't have to be so serious sounding. I am just speaking from my heart. This is where to start.

Me: Ok. From my heart, I feel fear. Fear that I will make mistakes that will hurt you. I want to give you a childhood that I did not have, a childhood where you can be whatever and whoever you want to be.

Sterling: Oh dad, you do this now. Oh sure you make mistakes. But, overall I feel very safe to be me, just me. I feel safe when I am with you. I feel your love flow through me. I feel like I can make

a mistake and you will still love me. Is this what you are trying to achieve?
Me: Yes! :-) I am pleased to hear you say this. But I can do better.
Sterling: Yes, dad, and you will, but you are doing so well now. I love you and feel loved by you. This is all that matters.
Me: I feel I could spend more time with you. I feel like I have been vacant this past year.
Sterling: You have been. I miss you. I miss your smile and attention. I miss seeing you happy. Is this because you don't have a job?
Me: In one way, yes. Having a job gave me structure and plenty of money.
Sterling: Money means a lot to you, doesn't it?
Me: I'm afraid so. I feel captive by it.
Sterling: I don't want to feel captive by money like that, but I haven't seen an example to be any other way.
Me: Me neither. What does your wisdom say?
Sterling: Do what you love, what gives you purpose. If money happens, great. If money doesn't, great!
Me: I'm afraid that the latter will happen.
Sterling: Then we can get a cheaper house, stop eating out. As long as we are together, I'm happy.
Me: I'm resisting this wisdom.
Sterling: Please don't. I'm only a child for this

moment. Please don't go chasing money anymore. I'm really not worried about it. Dad, what does money mean to you?
Me: That I was right. I measure my rightness by my money. I don't feel whole without it but I can't live without it. It is an addiction.
Sterling: You know what you did when I became addicted to Minecraft, right?
Me: Yes, I took it away for a while.
Sterling: Maybe you could take money away for awhile. That is how you chose your hobby to ride bikes and look how much you love it! You might want to try approaching your career in the same way: what do you love to do?
Me: I love spending time with you and your brothers.
Sterling: Then, start there.
Me: Thank you, son.
Sterling: Anytime, dad. Now, can we go play?
Me: Absolutely!

After writing during the workshop, we were asked to reread it and then write the emotions, thoughts, and/or body sensations we experiences while reading. The process is called feedback.

Feedback after rereading this entry:

There are themes I see in this dialogue that feel true:

1. Do what you love.
2. Do not let money guide you. Money may be an addiction. "Please don't go chasing money anymore."
3. Play.
4. Money may be an addiction to being seen as being right. The poor made mistakes. The rich made the "right" choices. Being right is so important to me.
5. Speak from my heart!
6. Notice the fear that blockades my well.
7. Place structure in your life.
   Daily meditation
   Going to bed at same time
   Turn TV off
   Read
   Just be.
8. Make a mistake and love yourself the same.

Themes: guilt, shame, regret, hope, vision, trusting, not running, accepting the unknown, gratitude to Sterling,

Day Three

"In order to grow within, an individual needs to conceive and carry out works outside of the self. These outer works thus derive their power from a source that is within the person; but the person draws the strength for his or her future growth from the very process by which he completes his work in a satisfying way. The work and the person, the artwork and the artist, in every field of activity, are thus in a mutually creative relation to each other. Each requires the other. Each has something to give to the other. Each has something to communicate to the other. The relation between a person and his work is a living expression of dialogue."

I chose to dialogue with Purpose:

Dialogue with Work/Purpose *August 20, 2013*

Purpose: Hello, Adam. It is me, Purpose. Are you there?

Me: Yes, I am listening.

Purpose: You sure do like me. I like being in you. You are a gift. I'm lucky to know you. But, I have a question, "Why don't we spend more time together?"

Me: Because you don't make money.

Purpose: That's interesting. Money means so much to you, doesn't it?

Me: Yes, I need it.

Purpose: For what?

Me: To live, to be happy.

Purpose: To be happy?

Me: I'm not sure about the "happy" part either.

Purpose: Again, "Why don't we spend more time together?"
Me: Because I am afraid of what others might think of me.
Purpose: Does that matter so much?
Me: Yes.
Purpose: And, what are you willing to sacrifice to ensure others like you? Purpose? You?
Me: I don't want to give you or money up.
Purpose: If you had to choose between money or me, which would you choose?
[a long pause ensued, and then]
Me: I choose you.
Purpose: Ok. When will you make that choice? You have been avoiding me and scared of me, haven't you?
Me: Yes, because I thought you would take my money.
Purpose: What about money means so much to you that you would consider sacrificing your own happiness?
Me: Safety. To not be controlled by others. So I can be me.
Purpose: Sounds like you often sacrifice being you in the hope of feeling safe and uncontrolled. But, then you can't be you. A dilemma.
Me: Yes, I sometimes think that I can temporarily choose money over purpose, so I can save up to then eventually choose purpose.
Purpose: Is this working for you?
Me: No way! No.
Purpose: Do you think it will eventually work for you?

Me: No, I have tried that path long enough to know this answer.
Purpose: Are you ready to choose purpose over money?
Me: Yes, But . . .
Purpose: "Yes, but" doesn't sound ready. It sounds like you want to keep trying the old way.
Me: NO. I'm just scared. I don't know where this will lead. But, I think if I don't try now, I will continue to compromise my integrity and this is more costly/painful than anything I've ever known.
Purpose: Are you ok?
Me: No, I'm fucking scared.
Purpose: Scared of what?
Me: Of making a mistake, of being a mistake.
Purpose: Which sounds like a bigger mistake, "1. Choosing money/safety over your purpose or 2. Choosing your purpose over safety?"
Me: I know continuing to choose money over purpose will extinguish my light.
Purpose: And, what does that feel like, extinguishing your light?
Me: Unbearable. Unconscious. No integrity.
Purpose: What now?
Me: I don't know.
Purpose: Try. What now?
Me: I could choose an activity or course and give everything to it. My time, attention, energy. Make it a priority.
Purpose: I am a gift. I want to be shared. But, mostly I

want to be with you often, frequently. You are a safe place.
Me: But, how can you say I am a safe place? I keep abandoning you.
Purpose: I understand your pain. I have been here your whole life. I have seen and felt your journey. You are safe because you are presence. You are energy. You are not your mind. Because I can see the future and you choose me more fully as you age. So, I am always here. Will never leave you even if you temporarily forget me. You are kind. You are beautiful. You are purpose. You are here. You have a vulnerability that I feel safe to be in. You always come back to me. I see you. I love you. I am you.
Me: What if I forget this moment?
Purpose: You are this moment. So, if you forget you'll eventually come back to it. And we can resume where you left off.
Me: That feels like unconditional Love. I can be here in this moment, here.
Purpose: Keep present and you will be whole because in this moment and at every moment, you are whole, love, presence.

Feedback: many tears.

Day Four

"Entrance Meditation...provides a neutral means by which we enter the deep and quiet place where our [self-]work is conducted. It is a means by which each person in their own rhythm enters their own psyche and proceeds inward until they come to a place that seems to them to have a quiet depth."[17]

Carol, the instructor, began the day standing in front of the class. Her sitting posture emanated a deep conviction as she began the class, "The body has the capacity to self-heal." Her voice, so clear and confident, gave me courage to keep diving into my well. She then read an Entrance Meditation called *Muddy/Clear: The Mirror of the Water* by Ira Progoff and instructed us to begin writing after we heard the words, "In the silence... In the silence."

With everyone sitting, their eyes closed and hands folded, she read slowly these words:

"I remember the saying
Of the old wise man, Lao Tse:
'Muddy water,
Let stand
Becomes clear.'

Thinking of that, I look within myself.
I see, On the screen of my mind's eye,
A stream of water, Moving, Swirling, Murky,
It is full of things.
I cannot look into this water.
I cannot see my reflection in this water.

Now the movement stops.
The water is in one place.
It is heavy colored, muddy
But it is becoming quiet; the water is at rest.
In its stillness the muddiness
Is settling to the bottom.

At the surface it becomes clear, Transparent.
I can see into the water more and more.
Now I can see through to the very depth of it.
There it shines and it reflects.

The heavens are reflected
In the quiet water.
It is clear.
I see the reflection of a tree in the quiet water.
The muddy water has become clear.

As I continue to look into the stillness
A reflection of myself
Begins to appear.
Deep in the quietness
Of the water, I see
A reflection of myself,
myself in many different forms.

I sit in the stillness
And let the images shape itself.

It becomes many things.
Many images appear in the still water,
Many things come up for me to see.

In the depth of the water, the images
that open the greatest vision within me
Are not those that are visible.
I do not see them; I just know them.
Something within me recognizes them
In the still water.

The muddy water has become quiet.
I sit gazing into it, seeing images,
Visible and invisible, letting them take form,
Letting them change and re-form themselves
In the depth of the still water,
In the mirror of the water,
In the depth of my Self,
Moving, moving,
In the Silence...In the Silence"[18]

Many images came up for me during this meditation. Without judgment or knowing what was going to happen after each word was written, I composed the following:

Entrance Meditation — *August 21, 2013*

In the forest, I stand behind a bush and look down. A brook flows under my feet.
In the water I see blood and follow the water up toward a clearing.

Light breaks through the tops of the tall trees to a large beast lying in the brook.

I see a white unicorn, wounded, bleeding. I watch from a distance behind a bush wondering what I can do. It thrashes. Vapor flowing from nostrils flaring. It has fight in it, but it is bleeding from its chest.

People walk by ignoring the magnificent being, bleeding, wounded. People walk by.

I know if I wait too long the unicorn will sleep, lose its fighting spirit, its will.

I'm shaking behind the bush.

I gather my courage. Breathing. Now. I'm stepping. Again, breathing. Now. I'm stepping.

Out into the clearing I slowly walk toward the unicorn.

The unicorn stops thrashing and stares into my eyes. It is reading my soul. It is calming down now.

I say in a whisper, "Breathing. Now. I'm stepping" and then step closer to the massive beast. The size of a clydesdale, I feel it's true nature, peace. Pure Peace.

I am afraid but I know what must be done.

I kneel beside the beast.

I bow my head and whisper, "Thank you for this opportunity."

The unicorn rests its head.

I place my hands on its gaping wound.

[My right writing hand began to tremble. I noticed I did not want to write the next words.]

I am a healer.

The unicorn is me and I am the unicorn.

In the silence. In the silence.

Feedback: Self-healing. Stepping forward with purpose. I feel grateful that I had the courage to write each word, even when I hesitated, hoping that the words would change if I held on to them long enough, I wrote them.

Day Five

"In those persons who have repressed their sorrow for many years, when they finally find a situation, as many do in the Journal Workshops, in which the open atmosphere gives them the inner freedom to let the crying happen, it is important that no one intrude. If we did intrude with our well-intentioned comforting, we would get into the other person's well. We would close it off at the point where it was freeing itself from the excess material so that it could regulate itself from within."[19]

This morning, Carol started the class by informing us that today we were to re-read our journal, to build up an energy, momentum. I felt like reaching for a seat belt.

I read through the journal. The momentum certainly happened, but I felt a dam in place. I felt very emotional to the point that while the day had just begun, I contemplated leaving the workshop. We were supposed to be writing but for the first time in the workshop nothing was happening for me. Nothing was writing.

I walked from my writing area to Carol, who was sitting at the front of the class, just sitting in silence, holding space for us. I told her I was feeling a strong urge to leave the workshop for the day and that I was overwhelmed with emotion. She calmly asked what was the one source of my emotions. I quickly answered, "Money."

She suggested I write 10 to 12 stepping stones of my relationship with money. My chest tightened. It was time to write and write I did.

I wrote 94 stepping stones. I missed lunch. I felt dizzy and disoriented.

I went back to Carol for guidance. She asked me when my relationship with money began. I said childhood. She recommended I choose one of the stepping stones. I chose being baptized at age seven.

She asked, "What was your sense of self?"

I paused, sat next to her, searching for an answer for what seemed like an hour. I then whispered to her with my voice cracking, "I had none. One was thrust upon me." She said to write that.

With pent up tears, I left the classroom with a pen and blank pages, found a nearby tree to lean into, and cried as I wrote:

Stepping Stone: Being Baptized at 7 *August 22, 2013*

At age 7, I didn't know who I was, but I knew what my father demanded I be: a Christian, embodying all of its doctrine, including and primarily hate, better than, anointed, chosen, special by being more special than others.

I felt pressured to act a certain way that properly reflected my closeness to God. I learned to act the part instead of being, inwardly, the part.

I was the oldest of eight, the example, the model, the experiment. My parents were desperate to make me, mold me.

I was voiceless. A puppet. A human program. I felt mindless. I felt alone. I felt emotionless, not allowed to show my emotions unless it was the emotion prescribed.

I felt mind-controlled. I believed God could hear my thoughts and, if they were sinful, God would tell my parents, my dad. So, I shut my mind off. No bad thoughts allowed. Suppressed my thoughts. Pushed them down. Ran away from them.

The atmosphere was stifling with always being around Christians from my cult church. Went to Christian school, surrounded by Christians. No place for mistakes.
God and money controlled the Universe. Money took second position to God. God allowed this as long as we

used our money with His will. If not, then He would take your money. Take everything that was important to you, including my own family.

Any loss or illness was a direct move that God allowed to punish/teach a lesson. The love God showed me was to not to send me to the hell, which I so obviously deserved.

I was a wretch. I deserved hell. When God wasn't enough to curb our behavior, my father used money, the "Money on the Wall".

I was a slave and I learned to serve two Masters: God and money. I became a fundamental Christian, investment banker. The apex of both God and money.

I felt like a prisoner in my own home, a tortured prisoner. Tortured at the deepest level of my soul.

I wept with grief in the acknowledgement of a childhood that was not of my choosing, difficult and harsh. I grieved in the arms of a tree, my tears from my well falling into the exposed roots, held safely.

Day Six

"In the course of the workshop we have an opportunity to write in the various sections of the Journal, and we are then invited to read. But no one is required to read.... We let each person follow the integrity of inner promptings.

We leave it to him or her to decide whether or not to read-now or later-and whether or not to speak in the workshop at all. We know that there may be experiences in a person's life that carry with them a great need to be spoken in the group."

That morning, before the workshop, I dialogued with the image that had haunted me for nearly three decades. When Carol asked if there was anyone who would like to read aloud something they had written, I realized what must be done.

I was drowning and in need of rescue again. I gulped. Water rushed into my throat. I raised my hand.

I explained to Carol and the group that I had drawn an image of a Devil Preacher and written a letter that morning to it. I raised to my feet, took the picture to the front of the room where an easel stood, placed the image on it and began to read in a slow rhythm:

Letter to Devil Preacher *August 23, 2013*

I see you, devil preacher, standing at your pulpit. Fire surrounding you. Fire to separate you from me.
You seem so strong, powerful, charismatic.
Do you know what you are? What you are doing to me?
What I let you do to me?

[I raised my hand, signaling to my witnesses that I needed a moment to breathe without speaking. My tears were choking me. My eyes so full of water, the image of the Devil Preacher became blurry to me. I could barely read the words on the page in my hands. But, I felt safe in this room full of strangers, each with their own tear-filled eyes. I continued slowly, pausing and resting after each word, my body visibly shivering.]

I am a child, open, curious, trusting.

I trust you to help me, guide me.

You take this role and I follow, following you to both places of light and dark.

You judge. You judge me. You say I am worthless, need a Savior, need you.

I trust you. You have been trusted by others. I follow the herd.

But, I look at you when you don't think you are being seen.

I see your real self.

Your humanness.

You are not God, simply a man, a boy in a man's body.

You believe what you do, what you say is truth. Well, that is what you project.

Inside you, there is much doubt, much fear. Fear.

You feel fear stronger than most. You seek God for solace.

You feel unworthy, unlovable, needing an outside Savior. This is the story your mind tells you. Heaven, the promise of

eternal life, the shortcut, the diversion from the inevitable, from certainty, death. You fear death, so you seek an alternative.
Your fear of death is so strong you must have followers, a herd, constantly telling you, "Thank you, you are so good, so close to God, I want to be like you." As long as there are followers, you will stay the course. Followers who share your fear of death.

Devil Preacher, I see you!

[I paused again because I wanted to make sure I meant what I was about to say to these witnesses. I paused as I was about to acknowledge the energy that propelled me to achieve a success that many have sought and few have seen. I heard my heart whisper, "Breathing. Now. I'm stepping." There was no holding down the truth any longer:]

Devil Preacher, I choose forgiveness.
[A long, painful sigh came out of my body, reminding me of my father's last, long exhale.]

I choose to see your essence, not the symptoms of your humanness.
I choose to forgive you.

[Another long pause and then]

I choose to love you.
I choose to see through you.

I cannot live fully until I see you, your essence. I need to live freely, free from the bounds of your ideas, your unchecked fears. You are a symptom, your fear is a symptom of non-acceptance, the non-acceptance of death.

I know your fear because I share your fear. But, I do not choose a fantasy ending in a place created by imagination/ survival. I choose ACCEPTANCE of my body's ensuing death. I, at times, too wish it were different by imagining an alternative.

Rest, breathe, be, Devil Preacher. Your work with me is complete.
Rest, breathe, be, Devil Preacher, it is time to accept our fate.

Namaste, Devil Preacher, I honor the spirit in you, which is also in me.

I sat down, placed my hands together under my chin in gratitude, and slowly nodded to the audience in the room to acknowledge their witness of my healing through vulnerability and authenticity. They answered my gratitude with compassionate smiles, prayerful hands, gracious bows, and watery eyes. I looked at the picture on the easel and saw the image begin to break into tiny square pieces, as the pieces swirled upward. And then the words were written on the blank page in front of me, "It is time to write the book."

Chapter 16
Masks Fall

I arrived home after the journal workshop knowing I had set out on a path that was no one else's but mine. There were many challenges ahead of me. The difference was that I had faced my strongest nemesis, the masks I believed protected me from being fully seen by others and, most important, by me, the masks that taught me to resist and resent the pain and suffering.

An immediate result of the workshop was a quieting of much of my negative self-talk. I had the newfound capacity to hear my heart's desire and I was no longer avoiding those giant leaps into fear-based lands. I was no longer defined by others, by the opinions on the Internet because I had seen me. I, too, had witnessed the man who publicly shared his struggle with past pain.

I now knew who Adam Smith was, something no one else could really give to or take from me. I no longer needed the security of hiding behind the name Mark, mistake, or hero. I shed the masks that kept the suffering alive. I found my passions. And I stepped back into my journey with a new appreciation for the lessons that simply being present in the journey can teach. I still wanted permanent, stable employment as money was continuing to dry up, but I also was grateful to have occasional part-time contract positions. I decided to live very simply, stop seeking CFO jobs while I wrote this book, and started building softer skills, skills that a traditional CFO would not have sought without the gift of change.

Over the following months, I took meaningful time out to be present and enjoy my family, began to deepen my mindfulness practice, enrolled in Essential Life Coach Training, and sought to teach what I had learned in a university setting.

Portland State University, after watching the YouTube protest video and the ensuing chaos, graciously gave me the opportunity to teach evening courses in Entrepreneurship and Finance. I was so afraid heading into that first class. I stood before fifty students who knew nothing about me. I had a choice to hide or expose. I had been hiding for so long, but since the journaling workshop, I knew that Adam Smith wanted, above all else, to live a life of authenticity, no matter the cost.

I began that first lecture, carefully choosing each word, making sure to stay scripted and free of anything that might tip someone off as to my public mistake. I felt tension inside still fearing that one student might just Google me right then and there and I would be called out publicly and probably get fired once again. I'd been there before.

I noticed my introduction to the course was dry and boring. It was lackluster and short on energy. A strength of mine is passion and I was restraining that because I was hiding. I paused. I looked at the class, full of glazed-over students. One student in particular named Henry was sitting in the last row with his head resting on his hand propped up by his elbow. He was looking at me, studying me. I took a deep breath and chose to tell my story. Childhood, chasing money, career, Chick-fil-A, the power of social media, and what I learned. All of it, much more condensed than this book, but the flow was there. I laid it out there for all to see, including how scared I was to share it with them. And you know what happened? Connection. Deep connection and respect. After class, most of the students lined up to tell me how excited they were to take the course. Henry gave me a high-five that wrapped into a hug and told me that at the beginning of the lecture he feared this was just going to be another boring class, but now, "Man, you be real and now you got my attention. Looking forward to the rest of the quarter, professor."

I'd let them in and they respected me for doing so. They were curious, full of questions. My passion returned and I taught entrepreneurship from a new, vulnerable place. I let Adam shine through and stepped out of my dark cave. I taught the whole semester from a place of authenticity. It was liberating. I was now writing a new chapter. I had a choice in how I was going to show up in the world, how I was going to *be* in the world. I did not have control over how people would react, but I had a choice and I'm glad I made the authentic one. My story was becoming a catalyst for change in people. If I had hidden it, tried to change it, or remained as Mark, I would've robbed myself and others of an opportunity to grow.

One of the most powerful moments of my de-masking journey was when a student came up to me at the end of the semester and she told me she needed to speak with me. I could see the emotion in her eyes and I knew she was afraid to say what she needed to say. I offered her a safe space to share. She began by saying that other students had advised her to remain quiet until grades were posted so she would not appear to be buttering me up in hopes for a better grade. She continued, "But, I don't care what grade you give me. When you first showed us your Chick-fil-A video, I was angry at you. So angry. I couldn't believe that Portland State would allow a horrible man like you to teach students. I judged you harshly without knowing you. And I was ready to walk out of that first class, but something in me told me to stay. I am so glad I listened. I became a better person because of this situation. You are a good, honest, authentic man, Adam, and I am so sorry that I misjudged you. I feel so guilty and ashamed that I did that. I am sorry for all that have judged you without knowing you." We both sat there crying. Authenticity and vulnerability had opened us up.

The next entrepreneurship course I taught integrated mindfulness. Mindfulness is essentially the moment-to-moment awareness of one's emotions, thoughts and sensations occurring in the present moment and is a transforming practice for anyone, including business leaders, to become leaders of our personal lives and the work for which we lead.

After my own experience of standing in front of an Entrepreneur Class and revealing myself as the person I had been hiding, I decided this level of vulnerability could free more than myself. I added a challenge to my students to become more vulnerable than they had comfortably ever been. During the last fifteen minutes of each class students met that challenge.

One student shared with the class through an intimate reciting of his first poem. Another exposed her fear that she had spent four years chasing a degree her parents wanted instead of the degree she wanted. One student performed an original love song while playing the guitar. Another shared his personal story of being incarcerated and how he had withheld that info from others for fear of being judged, a personal truth he had hidden for twenty years. There was a confession from a student that she was an alcoholic. Another female student, in a most vulnerable and moving revelation, told of her controlling mother who highly monitored her snacks as a child and expected an unachievable level of perfection that eventually drove this young woman to battle with anorexia and bulimia. She blasted down the dark doors of her cave when she shared her struggle to just eat three power bars a day in order to meet expectations. If that admittance wasn't vulnerable enough, she took it one step further and, in front of all fifty students, each a stranger, courageously shared her body measurement, with immense dignity and bravery. Every student's focus was on that young lady and she had never been more beautiful and accepted by herself than in that moment of raw vulnerability. That day, in that moment, she chose to take that challenge, turn on the lights, and let others see her without masks.

Students began shining the light on their

fears and waking up all around me. I taught the students that if they really wanted to do something interesting in business and get it funded, they could work harder than anyone, outsmart their competition, and hope to have some luck on their side, or they could look inward and listen to something deeper, something much wiser than their mind: their inner wisdom. We worked on finding out what these students really wanted and what really mattered in their lives. What doors did they want to knock down if fear was not a factor? What would they really like to see? And their resulting business ventures were beautiful.

Some of them were providing clean water in Africa. One woman wanted to build shelters for women, specifically women in South America. She was passionate about these women who were sex-trafficking victims, and she really wanted to put this program together. She went in to so much detail about it that by the end of the term it felt as if she had already built it. There was a student who had a brother with autism. She just wanted to help other people like her brother. She saw how society rejected her brother and how so many were unable to see the beauty, the gifts, the uniqueness these autistic people held and how they were just getting left behind, cast to the side. She got really hooked on life coaching and did a lot of it during the course. As a result she determined she was going to be a life coach for autistic people.

I still remember the time I asked the class, “So how was everyone’s weekend? Did you find anything you’re really interested in doing in your life?” She stood up and raised her hand so vigorously she was shaking. A young woman stood up in front of the class and let her heart out. She said that this was the most moving course for her. This class was the most important she’d taken because she found what she wants to do with her life. She talked for fifteen minutes, uninterrupted, about what that process was like, about searching, about how her parents wanted her to become a lawyer but she thought she wanted to study whale sharks, but she just kept digging deeper and deeper. And then there was this moment when she just met herself. She stood there describing this journey to everyone. And, of course, she’s crying and other people are watching, going “Wow, wow!” Hearing her speak from her heart with that much passion about her vision was an amazing learning experience for the other students who were asking themselves, *Is it really worth it? Do I really want to put in the time and effort to figure out what I really want to do in my life?*

I ended her public proclamation with, "See. See, that is what following your heart looks like. And for those who felt that emotion swell up inside you as you heard her speak her heart, that is what following your purpose feels like."

When you can actually see *purpose* on someone, you never forget it—the purpose that matches so clearly with what they ought to be doing, what they were born to do. What a teaching moment for those students . . . and for me.

Authenticity and vulnerability are the keys to unlock ourselves from the cages that were, intentionally and unintentionally built around us.

Chapter 17
The Wealth in Authenticity

For a full year after the chicken incident, I did not watch the YouTube video that at the time of this book's publication had over one million views. Up until the journal workshop, seeing the video would make my stomach nauseous. Remembering some of the phrases I spouted like, "I'm totally heterosexual...there's not a gay in me," can still bewilder me with how inarticulate I was. I intended to say that we don't need to be gay to stand up for gay rights. Many scoffers used this phrase to humiliate me. They said that I was obviously gay and afraid to admit it, which was meant to be an attack on my character as though being gay is something to be ashamed of.

A few months after the workshop, my wife and I noticed a pattern in one of our sons. He was having uncharacteristic and unpredictable, violent eruptions of emotion over conflict, big or small. After a few months of this behavior it was clear we needed to address it for the sake of the family's emotional balance. We tried exercise, time alone, meditation, taking away privileges, everything, but nothing seemed to work.

One evening, it was clear to us that he was

holding something in. Once you have experienced such suppression, you seem to be able to spot it in others much more easily. He and Amy went to a quiet place in his room. They sat on the bed and Amy told him what we had been noticing and that nothing seemed to be helping him with his anger.

"Is there something you want to tell me, something you have been hiding, son." And then just silence. Waiting.

His face grew red and fists clenched. He threw his hands over his face and buried his head under his blankets and began to weep. And then he reached for the words that would make my inarticulate protest now only partially true. He cried, "I'm gay."

Life is amazing when you step back and watch it. It is beautiful, full of poetry. This life became so much more interesting when I realized what was happening while I was botching a protest and struggling to find a job. Behind a young man voicing a truth that felt so foreign to say, there was a little boy watching his father stand up for other human beings who were viewed and treated as different. This little boy would watch and find the courage, not in his middle years of adulthood, but in his youth, to share his truth that so many would find fault with and use to shroud him in shame. This brave little boy would utter words that rendered our financial loss so inconsequential in comparison to the freedom he felt when he opened the door of his cave to someone with light and love who would just hold him and tell him he was going to be okay. He was going to be loved the same no matter what; he was accepted without conditions, laws, or prejudice.

I was wrong in the *way* I protested, and I was wrong about something else. There *was* a gay in me. And I am so grateful for the opportunity to love him, to support him, to walk with him, and whenever he needs it, to carry him. I love you, son, unconditionally.

This revelation was only the beginning of being able to watch the video of my protest and find beauty in the lessons it held instead of pain from the devastation and disruption it caused.

On self-awareness paths one begins to see deeper into one's present actions. One's past is up for review as well. I became aware of something that didn't look good, that I wanted to hide, from even myself. But while hiding is an historical habit of mine, the more recent and deeper freedom to simply watch myself, not in judgment but in love, allowed me to see something. I had been holding back love somewhere.

The day my dad signed those papers that moved me out of my siblings' presence was also the day my mother signed those same papers, and it was the day I emotionally separated from her. I put up a wall to keep her out of me.

After my father died and I began to earn the money that I so desperately wanted to make me whole, my mother would ask for help. I was hiding from myself the truth behind my "no." I had told her, "You need to work more hours before I start giving you money," or "If I give you money you are just going to give it to your Branham church." This was the rationale my mind generated to justify my refusal. What I realized, ironically at a time when I had no money to give, was that I was punishing her for not standing up to my dad, for not leaving him, and for not protecting us. I was holding back love to hurt her, to give her a taste of my resentment by denying her help. It was easier for me to give to a stranger than to the mother who healed while allowing a father to harm.

Recently, my mother, also the oldest of eight children attended the funeral of her brother, Robert. None of her children could make the funeral, none except me, as I was just a three-hour drive away and had no full-time job to keep me from the weekday funeral. She wasn't asking for money this time, just my presence.

There was no reason for denying her request or for the continued presence of the wall I'd had in place for so long. I took my oldest son, Sterling, and drove east past the waterfalls that flow into the Columbia River, from Portland to a tiny town in eastern Washington where her sister lived. I asked my mother if I could take her out for Mexican food—my mother's and my favorite cuisine. I knew she would say yes. I told her she could order anything she wanted. She ordered five sides of sour cream and four sides of guacamole. She scraped the ground beef out of her hard shelled tacos and mixed it with the ordered sides and began to eat this ad hoc dish. I knew she loved tacos, the crispiness, the oil, and the salt. But, today she left them on her plate.

I thought she was saving them for the end, the final best bites, but then I watched her mouth open as she ate and recalled the email request I'd received from her a year earlier. She needed money for dentures, but I was in no position to help at that point because I had my own family's financial needs to meet. For a moment I wished I had my money again.

The next morning my mother opened her bedroom door wearing a dark purple dress. She said it symbolized royalty, for Robert was with God now. She looked so sad and low as she thought about the first of her siblings she would have to say goodbye to today.

The dress that draped down to her ankles was a beautiful color. I walked toward her, stood facing her, and told her just that. She replied, "Thank you, honey. But, I just wish I wasn't so ugly. I wish I was young and pretty again like when your dad met me."

She'd never said something like this to me before. Her shoulders lowered and then her head as she looked down toward the ground. She was whimpering and I could feel love guide me. I put a hand on each of my mother's wet cheeks, my fingers touching her ears, my thumbs touching the tips of her lips. Her tears streamed into the spaces where my hands held her face. I leaned in and slowly kissed one wrinkle, the deepest one on her left cheekbone, and then another gently, and then another just as softly. I just kept kissing her withered face with my eyes open and my heart full.

I didn't see a mother. I saw a human being, standing in front of another human being, receiving love, compassion, forgiveness.

And all it cost was a million dollar cup of water. Thank you, universe, for this wonderful lesson you have taught me. Thank you for the wealth in authenticity.

I am grateful. So eternally grateful.

Chapter 18
Perfectly Imperfect

There's this strong urge in all of us to be perfect. Maybe it's all the perfect vacations, perfect fashions, perfect make-up, perfect smiles with perfect backgrounds of people living perfect lives that overwhelm us in media. Maybe the perfection urge is biological—a natural consequence of a species with ancestors that survived many dark nights in caves; a survival of the fittest, the most skilled, the most perfect at surviving.

But, we have taken this perfection skill into places of our lives that are unnecessary for survival, and in fact may now be detrimental to our survival. We have taken this perfection skill and pitted it against each other, where we must compare to feel complete. Perceived perfection demands we compare ourselves by finding what's *wrong* with others so we can feel more perfect than they, more complete, more worthy than they, and more acceptable to ourselves.

But, the temporary soothing we experience from this exercise is fleeting. For when we have pushed everyone around us to a perfectly, safe distance, we are left alone with just ourselves in our modern-day caves. And, like all perfectionists, once we have compared ourselves to others and found a story of either inferiority or superiority, we go for the jugular and compare ourselves to the fabricated and elusive idea of what we *should* look or *should* be like. We compare ourselves to a perceived, perfect version of us.

The goal of perfection starts with what is wrong with us and then how to change it without anyone knowing.

We are so consumed with maintaining the illusion of perfection that we can't ever risk someone seeing a chink in the armor, of realizing that for even one second we were anything but perfect. There is no room to be wrong, no room to admit we need any improvement, so we make our upgrades under cover, carefully picking apart every aspect of ourselves.

As we compare us to ourselves we eventually punish the imperfect us into submission, telling it to be better, smarter, prettier, more socially acceptable. But "fixing" all of those imperfections is not enough; we begin looking for other areas in need of improvement, other potential weaknesses and vulnerabilities that could pose a future threat to our perfection.

Everything is scrutinized over and over and we never allow ourselves just to be who we really are. The struggle for perfection will never end because nothing will ever be perfect enough. The programming from ceaseless, manipulative advertising, the message from the expectation of impossible standards, the wounding from hearing that we weren't good enough have deprived us of the ability to embrace our imperfections and limitations.

But there is a life-changing opportunity available in authenticity. There is a moment when we might actually hear ourselves thing or see ourselves write these tragic "truths" that come from realizing how we have picked ourselves apart, that we have torn ourselves down to the proverbial studs, and there is nothing left to criticize. It is at this authentic moment where we reach a dead end and there is no other choice but to turn around and make our way back, to begin rebuilding. If we can take an honest look at all the pieces of ourselves, of our lives that lie around us, there is a chance to start putting it all back together in a deliberate, albeit imperfect, way that reveals intention and awareness of the flaws. We recognize that our imperfection is beautiful. It is what makes us equal to each other, for when we are consciously starting from scratch with rebuilding we can see that all of us are working with the same raw materials. This is what allows us to truly connect with others at deep emotional, spiritual, and physical levels. When we have accepted our own imperfections we can acknowledge others' failed attempts of striving to have more, to be more, to be more worthy of love. We are able to be with others without wanting to change them or make them into something we think is better.

Recognizing the beauty in our imperfection is the way other people can sense something they recognize in themselves. The *unconditional acceptance* they sense from you creates connection, penetrating the walls they have spent so much time constructing for the same reasons you did: the desire to feel accepted just as we are, as perfectly imperfect as we are, right now, without any more striving or trying is one of the greatest freeing forces we know. Being our true, authentic, imperfect selves, without the masks is the gift that comes from enduring the pain of being laid bare and learning what matters most.

Epilogue

My journey continues. Sometimes it carries on in painful ways and sometimes in bliss. My truth is to accept it as it comes.

The Chick-fil-A media frenzy still affects my ability to find permanent work. In early 2014, I listened to my heart and spent six months building a career in corporate mindfulness only to learn weeks before getting our first big client that my online reputation was still in need of repair. The food stamps that humiliated me in childhood are now humbling and helping me in adulthood.

Amy has gone back to work as a Certified Veterinary Technician and is actively writing a children's book. Our boys are finally beginning to feel that life is stabilizing, and while the journey has been traumatizing and painful for them too, they have learned important lessons in unconditional love and acceptance.

Weeks before publishing this book, ABC's newsmagazine, 20/20, coincidentally called me to see what life was like for the "Chick-Fil-A guy." As absolutely terrifying as it was to get in front of a camera again without the ability to control what would be said and that was destined to go national again, I agreed to the interview because that's what I do now: I face the path I fear to take but know that which is mine.

Now with the book complete, I am ready to take the next step with an organization that values authentic leadership.

Above all else, I am wearing no masks. I am tempted to throw one on from time to time but have found absolute freedom in owning the truth of who I am. Fear of rejection and love of money no longer drive me. There's a light shining brightly on my shadows. And I am more passionate than ever about giving and receiving authentic vulnerability. In this journey, I have learned to love deeper and that came from learning to love myself first. My million dollar cup of water was a costly lesson—a lesson I would not have actively chosen. However, it is a lesson I was given, learned to accept, and eventually became truly grateful for. A lesson I would now choose a million times over. I'm thankful for the suffering that unlocked love. Goodbye million dollars, losing you gave me the freedom I sought through you. Losing you was worth every penny because losing you truly freed me.

Thank you for taking this journey with me. I hope you have found some of your own truths along the way. An authentic life, no matter how financially secure or insecure, is a rich life. Go ahead. Remove your masks. Live the life you were meant to live. And when you are drowning—because if you have a pulse you will find yourself drowning from time to time—remember to raise your hand above the treacherous waters. I guarantee you, there's an angel ready to rescue you. That angel may even be you.

ABOUT THE AUTHOR

Adam Mark Smith is simply like you, a human being. He listened to a voice within him to write this book, a book that crystallized the healing process of both an abusive and lovely childhood, his admirable business career, the global public shaming he endured after protesting for gay rights in a less than mindful manner, and what he learned when he finally accepted it all.

Adam loves dating his wife of 18 years and playing with his four sons by coaching their Little League teams, learning new tricks on the trampoline, riding bikes, wrestling, and falling off their skateboards.

Now currently looking for his next career opportunity, Adam has held various roles in investment banking, accounting, and corporate finance at companies, including Intel, DLJ LA, KPMG, IBM, and of course, Vante. He is a certified life coach, has taught courses at the University of Arizona and Portland State University, and holds an MBA and CPA.

Adam inspires others to lead their business and personal lives with authenticity, a heart of service, and courage to question their learned beliefs.

ACKNOWLEDGEMENTS

There have been countless people in my life who have supported me on the journey I call my own, too many to list them all individually here.

First, I am grateful for the families and organizations that were there for my siblings and me during our time of need. Thank you to the Hodges and Cordova families for bringing me into your homes. Thank you to Youth On Their Own and Clear Channel's Christmas Wish for your support. Thank you to the gentle and giving Joan Hills, who allowed me to work in her yard and with her animals while I was in high school and desperately needed funds to survive.

I am grateful for my therapists who provided a safe space for me to share. Thank you to Dr. Ron Wright in Tucson, Arizona for being the first man I could safely tell all my secrets and who introduced me to the transforming *Intensive Journal* workshop. Thank you to Dr. George Mecouch in Vancouver, Washington for his dream work, intuition, and guidance to draw the Devil Preacher. Thank you to Kenneth Andert in Portland, Oregon who currently witnesses the unfolding of this amazing life with me. Thank you to Dialogue House Associates and Jon Progoff, son of the late and revered Dr. Ira Progoff, who continues to champion the healing method of the *Intensive Journal* program.

Many thanks to the early review and feedback of the manuscript by Rebecca Strack at Held & Heard, Kristn Benke, editing by Cara Highsmith, and cover design by Mitchell Shea.

Thank you to the generous community of Portland, Oregon. To my mentor life coach, Randy Spelling of Being in Flow, you are a bright light. May your book, *Unlimiting You*, touch the world in the way your coaching has touched me. To my friend, John Andrew Williams, thank you for your generous offerings at Academic Life Coaching and Essential Life Coach Training. Thank you Jon Dickman for tutoring my children during this time and simply accepting dinner as payment, and to your lovely partner, Bob Wilson, who is a living example for me of Jesus and the Buddha.

Thank you to my sons, Sterling, Pierce, Sawyer, and Gibson, for your patience while I wrote this book. I am blessed to teach, hold, and love you during these precious childhood years. May you find this book a place of refuge when you need it most. And always, I love you no matter what, no matter who you become or what you do, I love you the same. Now let's go play!

And last, but certainly not least, I love and am

grateful for the angel I have had at my side during much of this journey. Amy, in addition to your many hours of editing, thank you for your laugh in the joy, light in the dark, and perseverance in the difficult. May we continue to flow with the never ending changes in this adventurous life. I love you, forever.

NOTES

1. www.wikipedia.com - William Marrion Branham (April 6, 1909 – December 24, 1965) was an American Christian minister, usually credited with initiating the post World War II healing revival.[1][2]
Branham's most controversial revelation was his claim to be the end-time "Elijah" prophet of the Laodicean church age.[3][4] His theology seemed complicated and bizarre to many people who admired him personally.[5] In his last days, Branham's followers had placed him at the center of a Pentecostal personality cult. Other than those that still follow him as their prophet, Branham has faded into obscurity.
2. "Blaise Pascal", Columbia History of Western Philosophy, page 353.
3. http://www.bpnews.net/38271
4. http://www.goodasyou.org/good_as_you/2012/07/audio-chickfila-president-coo-dan-cathy-says-arrogant-same-sex-marriage-shaking-fist-at-god-invites-god-judgment.html
5. http://www.bizjournals.com/atlanta/news/2012/08/03/vante-cfo-fired-for-rude-behavior-at.html
6. http://uanews.org/story/ua-statement-regarding-former-adjunct-lecturer-adam-smith
7. http://www.foxnews.com/us/2012/08/03/viral-video-man-picking-on-chick-fil-worker-gets-him-fired/
8. https://www.youtube.com/all_comments?lc=TDZTTtiFT2a7CFkpetELiryimSBLT5qSQBtJxpGZs-M&v=IZ2CNb2zkKg
9. http://www.theblaze.com/stories/2012/08/03/

exclusive-theblaze-interviews-the-guy-fired-for-berating-a-chick-fil-a-protester-employee/

10. www.milliondollarcupofwater.com

11. http://insider.foxnews.com/2012/08/07/chick-fil-a-employee-rachel-speaks-out-about-customers-inhumane-rant-i-forgive-adam-smith

12. http://www.foxnews.com/on-air/oreilly/index.html#/v/1785600545001/body-language-obama-vs-ryan/?playlist_id=86923

13. Ira Progoff (August 2, 1921 – January 1, 1998) was an American psychotherapist, best known for his development of the Intensive Journal Method while at Drew University. His main interest was in understanding the processes by which people develop which he formulated in his theories and approaches that he called holistic depth psychology. Dr. Progoff then implemented these theories in creating a practical method using an integrated system of writing exercises for ordinary people to develop themselves that is called the Intensive Journal method. He founded Dialogue House Associates in New York City to help promote this method.

Progoff began exploring psychological methods for creativity and spiritual experience in their social applications in the early 1950s. His doctoral dissertation in the field of the social history of ideas at the New School was on the work of C.G. Jung. In 1953, the dissertation was published in hardcover by the Julian Press as Jung's Psychology and its Social Meaning. Later editions were published by the Grove Press, Anchor/Doubleday, and Dialogue House. After receiving his doctorate, Progoff was awarded a Bollingen fellowship, and studied privately with Jung in Switzerland.

This work led to a reconstruction of depth psychology in

terms of the later work of Freud, Adler, Jung, and Rank in The Death and Rebirth of Psychology and a first statement of Holistic Depth Psychology in Depth Psychology and Modern Man. In 1963, Progoff put forward the method of Psyche-Evoking in The Symbolic and the Real.

In 1966, Progoff drew from the principles described in these books to introduce the Intensive Journal method of personal development, the innovation for which he is most remembered. This is a nonanalytic, integrative system for evoking and interrelating the contents of an individual life. Progoff wrote two books describing the method: At a Journal Workshop and The Practice of Process Meditation. The system's popularity spread rapidly.

As the public use of the method increased, the National Intensive Journal Program was formed in 1977. It supplied materials and leaders for the conduct of Intensive Journal workshops in the United States and other countries in cooperation with local sponsoring organizations.

Source: Wikipedia and Dialogue House Associates

14. At A Journal Workshop: Writing to Access the Power of the Unconscious and Evoke Creative Ability by Progoff, Ph.D., page 6

15. ibid, p. 12

16. ibid, p. 143

17. ibid, p. 225

18. The Well and The Cathedral: An Entrance Meditation, by Ira Progoff, PhD., (Dialogue House Library: NY) 1972, 1977, 1992 pp. 33-43.

19. Progoff, p. 39

20. ibid, p. 40